THE BILINGUAL SERIES OF
THE MOST IMPRESSIVE BEAUTY OF CHINA

风景名胜

FAMOUS SCENERY

主 编◎青 闰
副主编◎吕 苗 程 铭
参 编◎曹 阳 薛茜茜 张连亮

中国科学技术大学出版社

内容简介

"最美中国双语系列"是一套精品文化推广图书,包括《风景名胜》《民俗文化》《饮食文化》《杰出人物》《科技成就》《中国故事》六册,旨在传播中华优秀文化,传承中华民族宝贵的民族精神,展示奋进中的最美中国,可供广大中华文化爱好者、英语学习者及外国友人参考使用。

本书介绍了中国部分代表性的自然景观与人文景观,展示了中国的辽阔疆域与大好河山。

图书在版编目(CIP)数据

风景名胜:英汉对照/青闰主编.—合肥:中国科学技术大学出版社,2021.11

(最美中国双语系列)

ISBN 978-7-312-05207-1

Ⅰ.风… Ⅱ.青… Ⅲ.风景名胜区—介绍—中国—汉、英 Ⅳ.K928.7

中国版本图书馆CIP数据核字(2021)第122418号

风景名胜
FENGJING MINGSHENG

出版	中国科学技术大学出版社 安徽省合肥市金寨路96号,230026 http://press.ustc.edu.cn https://zgkxjsdxcbs.tmall.com
印刷	合肥市宏基印刷有限公司
发行	中国科学技术大学出版社
经销	全国新华书店
开本	880 mm×1230 mm 1/32
印张	7
字数	169千
版次	2021年11月第1版
印次	2021年11月第1次印刷
定价	35.00元

前　言　Preface

文化是一个国家与民族的灵魂。"最美中国双语系列"旨在弘扬和推广中华优秀文化，突出文化鲜活主题，彰显文化核心理念，挖掘文化内在元素，拓展文化宽广视野，为广大读者了解、体验和传播中华文化精髓提供全新的视角。本系列图书秉持全面、凝练、准确、实用、自然、流畅的撰写原则，全方位、多层面、多角度地展现中华文化的源远流长和博大精深，对于全民文化素质的提升具有独特的现实意义，同时也为世界文化的互联互通提供必要的借鉴和可靠的参考。

"最美中国双语系列"包括《风景名胜》《民俗文化》《饮食文化》《杰出人物》《科技成就》《中国故事》六册，每册中的各篇文章以文化剪影为主线，以佳句点睛、情景对话和生词注解为副线，别出心裁，精彩呈现中华文化的方方面面。

"最美中国双语系列"充分体现以读者为中心的编写理念，从文化剪影到生词注解，读者可由简及繁、由繁及精、由精及思地感知中国文化的独特魅力。书中的主线和副线是一体两面的有机结合，不可分割，如果说主线是灵魂，副线则是灵魂的眼睛。

"最美中国双语系列"的推出，是讲好中国故事、展现中国立场、传播中国文化的一道盛宴，读者从中可以感悟生活。

《风景名胜》分为自然景观和人文景观两大部分，这里有"五岳之尊"泰山，有"天下第一奇山"黄山，有"天然植物园"神农架，有瑰丽奇绝的丹霞地貌,也有全球最大、最完整的四川大熊猫栖息地,有"一山分四季,十里不同天"的红河哈尼梯田,有世界第一高峰珠穆朗玛峰,有"天然画廊"和"人间仙境"长江三峡,有"世界奇迹"万里长城,有"皇家园林"颐和园,有"人间天堂"杭州西湖,有"天下第一仙山"武当山,有"世界第八大奇迹"秦陵兵马俑,还有"天下第一名刹"少林寺……可谓流光溢彩,精彩纷呈。

本书由焦作大学吕苗、焦作师范专科学校曹阳撰写初稿,南京大学程铭、郑州郑东新区龙翔学校薛茜茜撰写二稿,焦作大学张连亮撰写三稿,焦作大学青闰负责全书统稿与定稿。

最后,在本书即将付梓之际,衷心感谢中国科学技术大学出版社的大力支持,感谢朋友们的一路陪伴,感谢家人们始终不渝的鼓励和支持。

青 闰

2021年3月6日

目 录 Contents

前言 Preface ·· i

第一部分 自然景观
Part I Natural Landscape

泰山 Mount Tai ··· 003
黄山 Yellow Mountain ·· 009
神农架 Shennongjia ··· 015
武陵源风景名胜区 Wulingyuan Scenic and Historic Interest
　Area ·· 020
武夷山 Mount Wuyi ··· 026
梵净山 Mount Fanjing ·· 032
中国丹霞地貌 Danxia Landform in China ······························· 038
中国南方喀斯特 South China Karst ······································ 044
黄龙寺-九寨沟风景名胜区 Huanglong Temple and
　Jiuzhai Valley Scenic and Historic Interest Area ···················· 050
四川大熊猫栖息地 Sichuan Giant Panda Habitats ···················· 056
云南三江并流保护区 Three Parallel Rivers Protected Region
　in Yunnan ·· 062

风景名胜

红河哈尼梯田　Red River Hani Terraces ··············068

可可西里自然保护区　Hoh Xil Nature Reserve ··············074

珠穆朗玛峰　Mount Qomolangma ··············080

新疆天山　The Tianshan Mountains in Xinjiang ··············086

长江三峡　The Three Gorges of the Yangtze River ··············091

西湖　The West Lake ··············096

庐山　Mount Lu ··············101

五台山　Mount Wutai ··············106

第二部分　人文景观
Part II　Cultural Landscape

长城　The Great Wall ··············113

故宫　The Imperial Palace ··············118

颐和园　The Summer Palace ··············123

天坛　The Temple of Heaven ··············128

避暑山庄　The Imperial Mountain Summer Resort ··············134

孔庙、孔府和孔林　The Confucian Temple, Mansion and Graveyard ··············139

苏州古典园林　Suzhou Classical Gardens ··············144

武当山古建筑群　The Ancient Building Complex in Mount Wudang ··············149

云冈石窟　The Yungang Grottoes ··············154

秦始皇陵及兵马俑　The Mausoleum of the First Emperor of Qin

目 录

and Terracotta Warriors ·················159

少林寺　Shaolin Temple ·················164

龙门石窟　The Longmen Grottoes ·················169

青城山和都江堰　Mount Qingcheng and Dujiangyan
　　Irrigation System ·················175

峨眉山和乐山大佛　Mount Emei and Great Buddha in Leshan ······180

大足石刻　Dazu Rock Carvings ·················185

莫高窟　The Mogao Grottoes ·················190

丽江古城　The Old Town of Lijiang ·················195

拉萨布达拉宫历史建筑群　The Historic Complex of
　　the Potala Palace in Lhasa ·················200

鼓浪屿国际历史社区　Gulangyu International Historical
　　Community ·················205

澳门历史城区　The Historic Center of Macao ·················210

第一部分 自然景观

Part Ⅰ Natural Landscape

泰山

Mount Tai

导入语　Lead-in

泰山，古称"岱山"，春秋时期始称"泰山"。自汉代以来，人们把东岳泰山、南岳衡山、西岳华山、北岳恒山和中岳嵩山合称为"五岳"，其中泰山享有"五岳之尊"的美誉。泰山位于山东省泰安市

和济南市境内，主峰玉皇顶海拔1545米，南麓始于孔子故里曲阜，北麓止于泉城济南。泰山是世界首例文化与自然双重遗产、首批国家级风景名胜区、世界地质公园，它将历史文化与自然景观和谐地融合在一起，被誉为中国历史文化的缩影和中华民族精神的象征。

风景名胜

文化剪影　Cultural Outline

Mount Tai amazes the world by virtue of its features of being majestic, fantastic, **precipitous**①, beautiful, **secluded**② and profound. You can not only appreciate the magical beauty of nature, but also enjoy the historical and cultural prosperity from Mount Tai, which has always been the spiritual source of Chinese artists and scholars, as well as the symbol of ancient Chinese civilization and belief.

泰山以雄、奇、险、秀、幽、奥等特色而著称。在泰山,你不仅可以领略大自然的神奇之美,也可以饱览历史文化之盛。泰山历来都是中国文人墨客的精神源泉,也是古代中国文明和信仰的象征。

Mount Tai, located on the vast North China Plain, is famous for its **grandeur**③ and naturally has been an object of worship. For thousands of years many emperors paid their **homage**④ to the Mount Tai, expressing gratitude to heaven and earth with sacrifice and worship. Ancient literati even admired Mount Tai, and they came to visit and write poems and prose. Among them the humanistic masterpieces and the natural landscapes are perfectly integrated in harmony.

泰山地处广阔的华北平原,以雄伟壮观而闻名,因此成为人们崇拜的对象。古代帝王对泰山的崇拜绵延几千年,他们在泰山封禅、祭祀,以谢天地恩泽。古代的文人雅士更是对泰山仰慕备至,纷纷前来游历并作诗记文,其人文杰作与自然景观完美和谐地融为一体。

Mount Tai Scenic Area is the most famous for its Sunrise, Cloud Sea Jade Plate, Sunset Glow and Yellow River Golden Belt. Visitors can go up the mountain by cableway or hike to get close to nature. Mount Tai is the only famous mountain that received the emperor's worship; and it is regarded as a precious heritage by people all over the world because of the integration of its unique humanistic **connotation** and natural landscape.

泰山风景区以日出、云海玉盘、晚霞夕照和黄河金带著称。游客可乘坐索道上山,或是徒步攀爬以亲近自然。泰山是唯一受皇帝封禅的名山,因其独特的人文内涵与自然景观的融合而被世界各国人民视为珍贵的遗产。

 佳句点睛 Punchlines

1. The unique geographical position of Mount Tai has created its **supreme** position.
泰山地理位置独特,造就了其至尊的地位。

2. Mount Tai has been the spiritual driving force of the national progress and development with its height and grandeur.
泰山因其高大、雄浑的山形而成为国家进步发展的精神动力。

3. Mount Tai has witnessed the development of the national spirit and become the carrier of the spiritual culture of Chinese civilization.

泰山见证了民族精神的发展历程,成为中华文明的精神文化载体。

情景对话 Situational Dialogue

A: I've heard you're going to China next week?

B: Yeah, I'm looking forward to that! You know it took me about a month to plan this trip.

A: How long are you gonna stay there?

B: I'll stay in Shandong for one week and then a couple of days in Dalian.

A: Oh, it's a good idea.

B: By the way, would you like to tell me about Mount Tai?

A: Sure! There're seventy-two majestic peaks, magnificent waterfalls, centuries-old pines and **cypresses**⑦ and fascinating rocks in Mount Tai.

B: And then?

A: There're five tourist zones and two routes up the mountain—one in the east and other in the west. Mount Tai is one of the birthplace of early Chinese civilization and its surrounding area is one of the ancient political, economic and cultural centers, where a lot of precious cultural relics are **preserved**⑧.

B: Thank you for telling me these.

A: My pleasure.

A: 我听说你下周要去中国?

B: 是的,我很期待! 我花了大约一个月时间来计划这次旅行。

A: 你打算在那里待多久?

B: 我打算在山东待一周,然后在大连待几天。

A: 噢,这主意不错。

B: 对了,你愿意给我讲讲泰山吗?

A: 当然可以,泰山有七十二座雄伟的山峰、壮观的瀑布、古老的松柏和迷人的岩石。

B: 还有呢?

A: 还有五个旅游区和两条上山的路线——一条在东部,一条在西部。泰山是中国古代早期文明的发祥地之一,周边地区是古代政治、经济、文化中心之一,那里保存有大量珍贵的文物。

B: 谢谢你告诉我这些。

A: 不客气。

生词注解 Notes

① precipitous /prɪˈsɪpɪtəs/ *adj.* 险峻的;急转直下的

② secluded /sɪˈkluːdɪd/ *adj.* 隐蔽的;隐居的

③ grandeur /ˈɡrændʒə(r)/ *n.* 宏伟;壮观

风景名胜

④ homage /ˈhɒmɪdʒ/ *n.* 敬意;尊敬

⑤ connotation /ˌkɒnəˈteɪʃn/ *n.* 内涵;隐含意义

⑥ supreme /suːˈpriːm/ *adj.* 至高的;最重要的

⑦ cypress /ˈsaɪprəs/ *n.* 柏树;柏木属植物

⑧ preserve /prɪˈzɜːv/ *vt.* 保存;保护

黄山

Yellow Mountain

 导入语 Lead-in

黄山,原名"黟山",唐朝时更名为"黄山",意为"黄帝之山"。黄山是中国十大风景名胜之一,以奇松、怪石、云海、温泉而驰名,被誉为"天下第一奇山"。徐霞客曾两次游览黄山,并赞叹道:"薄海内外,无如徽之黄山。登黄山,天下无山,观止矣!"黄山享有"五岳归来不看山,黄山归来不看岳"的美誉。黄山的自然美使历代文人骚客沉醉其中,留下了无数的不朽佳作,如徐霞客的《游黄山日记》、袁牧的《游黄山记》、叶圣陶的《黄山三天》、丰子恺的《上天都》等,都完美记叙了黄山的绝美风光。黄山哺育了世世代代的艺术家,艺术家们又赋予了黄山艺术生命。黄山是世界文化与自然双重遗产、世界地质公园和国家5A级旅游景区。

文化剪影 Cultural Outline

Yellow Mountain, located in Huangshan City in the south of Anhui Province, covers an area of 160.6 square kilometers, with thousands of peaks **contending**① for beauty, and there are mainly 72 majestic peaks, among which the **altitude**② of the three main peaks— "Lotus Peak" "Bright Summit" and "Heavenly Capital Peak" are above 1,800 meters. Yellow Mountain starts from Huangshi in the east to Xiaolingjiao in the west, and from Erlong Bridge in the north to Tangkou Town in the south. It is divided into 9 scenic areas, including Wenquan, Yungu, Yuping, Beihai, Songgu, Diaoqiao, Fuxi, Yanghu and Fugu, with more than 200 **attractions**③.

黄山位于安徽省南部黄山市境内,核心景区面积160.6平方千米,千峰竞秀,主要有七十二雄峰,其中莲花峰、光明顶和天都峰三大主峰的海拔都在1800米以上。黄山东起黄狮,西至小岭脚,北白二龙桥,南达汤口镇,分为温泉、云谷、玉屏、北海、松谷、钓桥、浮溪、洋湖和福固9大景区,200多个景点。

Yellow Mountain combines the charm of China's famous mountains, with the majesty of Mount Tai, the **precipitousness**④ of Mount Hua and the smoky clouds of Mount Heng, as well as the flying waterfalls of Mount Lu, the strange stones of Mount Yandang and the beauty of Mount Emei. It is known as "The Most Wonderful Mountain in China".

黄山集中国名山魅力于一体,既有泰山的雄伟、华山的险峻、衡山的烟云,又有庐山的飞瀑、雁荡山的奇石和峨眉山的秀丽,被誉为"天下第一奇山"。

With its unique charm, Yellow Mountain is well known all over the world for its various green pines, exquisite **grotesque** rocks, ever-changing sea of clouds and refreshing hot springs.

黄山具有独特的魅力,以千姿百态的苍松、玲珑别透的怪石、变化无穷的云海和沁人心脾的温泉而闻名于世。

佳句点睛 Punchlines

1. Xu Xiake, a geographer of the Ming Dynasty, visited Yellow Mountain on two occasions, **gasping** in admiration, "Once climbing the summit of Yellow Mountain, you can cease visiting because you find no other mountain can match for it."

明朝地理学家徐霞客曾经两游黄山,赞叹道:"登黄山,天下无山,观止矣。"

2. Yellow Mountain combines its natural landscape with humanistic connotation, forming a part of Chinese unique culture.

风景名胜

黄山将自然景观与人文内涵相结合,形成了中国特色文化的一部分。

3. The sea of clouds over Yellow Mountain is one of the most spectacular, with clouds and mist drifting all over the sky with the wind, sometimes rising, sometimes falling, sometimes whirling or sometimes stretching, forming a **kaleidoscope**⑦ of ink and cloud paintings.

黄山云海堪称一绝,漫天云雾随风飘移,时而上升,时而下坠,时而回旋,时而舒展,构成一幅幅变化万千的云海水墨画。

情景对话 Situational Dialogue

A: Glad to meet you here. Where are you going now?

B: I'm going to the railway station to buy a ticket.

A: Oh, really? What a **coincidence**⑧! Me too.

B: The National Day holiday is coming. Do you have a plan for it?

A: Yes. I'll travel to Anhui to enjoy the charming Yellow Mountain.

B: Yellow Mountain? I've heard of it from my friend. Would you like to tell me about it?

A: Sure. It's China's one of the top tourist mountains, where there're 72 majestic peaks, as well as strange pines, grotesque rocks, cloud seas and hot springs. In addition to the wonderful natural landscape, it is a rich art treasure, where the scholars and artists of all ages have left countless great works of literature while enjoying the beautiful scenery.

B: Oh, how great! Could I go with you?

A: Certainly.

A: 很高兴在这里见到你。你这是要去哪?

B: 我去火车站买票。

A: 是吗? 太巧了,我也是去买票。

B: 国庆假期马上到了,计划好去哪里了吗?

A: 是的,我要去安徽游览迷人的黄山。

B: 黄山? 我听朋友讲过。你愿意给我介绍一下吗?

A: 当然。黄山是中国旅游胜地之一,那里有七十二雄峰,还有奇松、怪石、云海和温泉。除了奇绝的自然山水之外,黄山还是一座丰富的艺术宝库,历代文人雅士在观赏美景的同时留下了无数文学佳作。

B: 噢,太棒了! 我能和你一起去吗?

A: 当然可以。

生词注解 Notes

① contend /kən'tend/ vi. 竞争;抗衡

② altitude /'æltɪtjuːd/ n. 海拔;高地

风景名胜

③ attraction /əˈtrækʃn/   n. 游览胜地；吸引力

④ precipitousness /prɪˈsɪpɪtəsnəs/   n. 险峻；陡峭

⑤ grotesque /grəʊˈtesk/   adj. 奇形怪状的

⑥ gasp /gɑːsp/   vi. 喘着气说话；喘息

⑦ kaleidoscope /kəˈlaɪdəskəʊp/   n. 万花筒；千变万化

⑧ coincidence /kəʊˈɪnsɪdəns/   n. 巧合；同时发生

神农架

Shennongjia

导入语 Lead-in

神农架,全称神农架林区,位于湖北省西部,东起保康,西至巫山,南依兴山、巴东,濒临三峡,北靠房县、竹山,贴近武当,地处北亚热带季风气候区,被称为"华中屋脊"。传说神农架是华夏始祖神农炎帝搭架采药、治病救人、引导耕作的地方。神农架凭借得天独厚的地理位置和自然环境保存着中国中部地区最大的原始森林,享有"绿色明珠"和"天然植物园"的美誉。2016年,神农架被联合国教科文组织列入《世界自然遗产名录》,神农架的文化生态与自然生态一样丰富,具有经久不衰的无穷魅力。

风景名胜

文化剪影 Cultural Outline

Shennongjia is also known as the "Roof of Central China", because the highest peak in Shennongjia—Shennong Peak is 3,105.4 meters above sea level, the first peak in Central China and also the dividing crest between the Yangtze River and the Han River. Shennongjia is the only **oasis**① in China that is well-preserved inland and the only green treasure in the world's mid-**latitude**② regions and also a large-scale natural medicine storehouse.

神农架被誉为"华中屋脊",因其最高峰——神农顶海拔高达3105.4米,是华中第一峰,也是长江与汉江的分水岭。神农架是我国内陆唯一保存完好的绿洲和世界中纬度地区唯一的绿色宝地,也是规模宏大的天然药材库。

With its excellent geographical location and natural **environment**③, Shennongjia still **preserves**④ the peculiar features of **primitive**⑤ forests to this day, so many rare animals and plants can reproduce here.

神农架凭借优越的地理位置和自然环境,至今依然较好地保存着原始森林的特有风貌,因此多种珍稀动植物得以在此繁衍。

Shennongjia is one of the birthplaces of Bachu culture, and also the place where Yinshang culture, Qinhan culture, Bashu culture and

Jingchu culture meet. The precious creation **epic**⁶ *Legend of Darkness*, the beautiful folk songs and colorful legendary stories form the treasure house of Shennongjia's folk literature.

神农架是巴楚文化的发祥地之一,也是殷商文化、秦汉文化、巴蜀文化和荆楚文化的汇聚地。弥足珍贵的创世史诗《黑暗传》、优美动听的民间歌谣和绚丽多彩的传说故事构成了神农架的民间文学宝库。

佳句点睛 Punchlines

1. Shennongjia presents us with an **antique**⁷ landscape painting based on its unique landform.

神农架以其独特的地貌为我们呈现出一幅古色古香的风景画。

2. Shennongjia has the only well-preserved subtropical forest ecosystem in the mid-latitudes of the world today.

神农架拥有当今世界中纬度地区唯一保存完好的亚热带森林生态系统。

3. The Shennong Altar is the core part of the Shennongjia scenery, which is a place specially for the **descendants**⁸ of Yan and Huang to remember their **ancestors**⁹ and worship the gods.

神农坛是神农架景区的核心,是专供炎黄子孙缅怀先祖和祭祀神灵的场所。

风景名胜

 情景对话 **Situational Dialogue**

A: Today we'll learn about Shennongjia.

B: Shengnongjia?

A: Yes. First, we'll appreciate its beautiful scenery.

B: Wow, what beautiful scenery! I really wanna see this mysterious and fascinating place!

A: Shennongjia is located in the southwest of Hubei Province, with a scenic area of 3,250 square kilometers. It still preserves the peculiar features of the virgin forest, so many rare animals and plants **multiply**① here. Besides, it's also a large-scale natural medicine storehouse.

B: If we have a chance to travel, we'll take good care of this primitive scenic area.

A: Well said. Shennongjia is the only well-preserved oasis in China and the only green treasure in the world's mid-latitude regions.

B: So we'll surely protect it.

A：今天我们一起来了解一下神农架。

B：神农架？

A：是啊。首先，我们先欣赏一下神农架景区的美景。

B：哇，好漂亮的风光！我真想去看看这个神秘迷人的地方！

A：神农架位于湖北省西南部，景区面积3250平方千米。神农架至今还较好地保存着原始森林的特有风貌,因此多种珍稀动植物得以在此繁衍。此外,神农架也是一座规模宏大的天然药材库。

B: 如果有机会去旅游,我们要好好爱护这片原始景区。

A: 说得好。神农架是我国内陆唯一保存完好的绿洲和世界中纬度地区唯一的绿色宝地。

B: 我们一定要好好保护它。

生词注解 Notes

① oasis /əʊˈeɪsɪs/ *n.* 绿洲;舒适的地方

② latitude /ˈlætɪtjuːd/ *n.* 纬度;范围

③ environment /ɪnˈvaɪrənmənt/ *n.* 环境;生存环境

④ preserve /prɪˈzɜːv/ *vt.* 保存;保护

⑤ primitive /ˈprɪmətɪv/ *adj.* 原始的;远古的

⑥ epic /ˈepɪk/ *n.* 史诗;史诗体裁

⑦ antique /ænˈtiːk/ *adj.* 古老的;年代久远的

⑧ descendant /dɪˈsendənt/ *n.* 后裔;子孙

⑨ ancestor /ˈænsestə(r)/ *n.* 始祖;祖先

⑩ multiply /ˈmʌltɪplaɪ/ *vi.* 繁殖;增加

武陵源风景名胜区

Wulingyuan Scenic and Historic Interest Area

 导入语　Lead-in

　　武陵源风景名胜区地处中亚热带山原型季风性湿润气候区,溪流淙淙。武陵源独特的石英砂岩峰林世所罕见,石英砂岩山峰多达3103座,层峦叠嶂,云雾缭绕,云海时浓时淡,石峰若隐若现,似神若仙,姿态万千,如人间仙境。1984年,张家界、索溪峪和天子山三大景区被命名为"武陵源"。武陵源于1988年被列入第二批国家重点风景名胜区,1992年被联合国教科文组织列入《世界自然遗产名录》,2004年被列为中国首批世界地质公园,2007年被列入中国首批国家5A级旅游景区。

文化剪影 Cultural Outline

Wulingyuan Scenic and Historic Interest Area include Zhangjiajie Forest Park, Suoxiyu Nature Reserve and Mount Tianzi Nature Reserve. It not only has layers of ridges, endless quartz sandstone peaks, **spectacular**① distinctive karst caves and colorful rare geology relic landscape, but also rich plant resources and valuable wild rare animals.

武陵源风景名胜区包括张家界森林公园、索溪峪自然保护区和天子山自然保护区。它既有层峦叠嶂、连绵不断的石英砂岩峰林，又有蔚为壮观、特色鲜明的溶洞和丰富多彩的珍奇地质遗迹景观，也有丰富的植物资源和宝贵的野生珍稀动物。

Located in the middle of Wuling Mountain, Zhangjiajie is China's first national forest park, where there is unique varied landforms and lush trees, surrounded by mountains, deep slopes and steep **ravines**②, and cloaked with a warm and humid climate. Waterfalls, springs, streams, ponds and lakes are dotted all over Zhangjiajie, wonderfully created by nature. There are many scenic spots, especially indescribably wonderful Huangshizhai, Shadaogou, Jinbian Rock and Jinbian Brook.

张家界地处武陵山中，是中国第一个国家森林公园，其地貌奇特，树木茂盛，山地环抱，坡陡沟深，气候暖湿。瀑、泉、溪、潭、湖遍布其间，妙趣天成。张家界景点众多，黄狮寨、砂刀沟、金鞭岩和金鞭溪更是妙不可言。

风景名胜

The weather in Wulingyuan is colorful and varied. The most common **meteorological**① wonders include five forms such as cloud-and-mist, cloud-sea, cloud-wave, cloud-**cascade**① and clouds. Peaks loom in the vast sea of clouds, like Penglai Fairy Island, sometimes the cloud-sea brimming over the peak and rolling down in a landslide into the flying cloud-cascade.

武陵源的气象景观多姿多彩，变化万千。最常见的气象奇观有云雾、云海、云涛、云瀑和云彩五种形态。群峰在茫茫云海中若隐若现，犹如蓬莱仙岛，有时云海漫过峰顶，以排山倒海之势滚滚而下，化为飞天云瀑。

佳句点睛 Punchlines

1. The landscape of Mount Tianzi is created by nature, without any trace of **artificiality**①.

天子山的风景都是天造地设，没有任何人工雕琢的痕迹。

2. Huanglong Cave in Suoxi Valley is a **microcosm**① of the karst landscape of Southeast Asia.

索溪峪黄龙洞是东南亚岩溶景观的缩影。

3. Wuling Pines enjoy the reputation that "there're three thousand peaks in Wulingyuan, one hundred and eight thousand pines on these peaks."

武陵松享有"武陵源里三千峰,峰有十万八千松"的美誉。

情景对话 Situational Dialogue

A: Do you know anything about Wulingyuan?

B: I know something about it.

A: Do you know the features of Wulingyuan, then?

B: It's a long story. Hundreds of millions of years ago, Wulingyuan was a vast ocean. Today, it is famous for its "five wonders".

A: Which "five wonders"?

B: They're **fantastic**⑦ peaks, strange rocks, **dells**⑧, lovely waters and karst caves.

A: Really wonderful. What else?

B: There're **ethnic**⑨ minorities such as Tujia, Miao and Bai, whose folkways and customs are simple and unique, just like a paradise in the world.

A: I've heard that there was a great writer coming out here.

B: Yes, he was Shen Congwen, who was the father of local literature.

A: I read his works such as ***Recollections***⑩ ***of West Hunan*** and ***Border Town***. Reading his works is like stepping into this side of paradise.

B: That's right.

风景名胜

A: 你对武陵源了解吗?

B: 略知一二。

A: 那你知道武陵源有哪些特色吗?

B: 说来话长,亿万年前,武陵源还是一片汪洋大海。现在的武陵源以"五绝"闻名于世。

A: 都是哪"五绝"?

B: 奇峰、怪石、幽谷、秀水和溶洞。

A: 确实够绝的。还有呢?

B: 这里居住着土家族、苗族、白族等少数民族,他们民风淳朴,风俗独特,这里就像世外桃源一般。

A: 我听说这里走出了一位大作家。

B: 没错,他就是乡土文学之父沈从文。

A: 我读过他的《湘西散记》和《边城》,读他的作品就像走进了人间天堂。

B: 这话不假。

生词注解 Notes

① spectacular /spekˈtækjələ(r)/ *adj.* 壮观的;引人入胜的

② ravine /rəˈviːn/ *n.* 沟壑;山涧

③ meteorological /ˌmiːtiərəˈlɒdʒɪkl/ *adj.* 气象的;气象学的

④ cascade /kæˈskeɪd/ *n.* 小瀑布;瀑布状物

⑤ artificiality /ˌɑːtɪˌfɪʃiˈæləti/ *n.* 人工;人造物

⑥ microcosm /ˈmaɪkrəʊkɒzəm/ *n.* 缩影;微观世界

⑦ fantastic /fænˈtæstɪk/ *adj.* 极好的;极出色的

⑧ dell /del/ *n.* 幽谷;长着树林的山谷

⑨ ethnic /ˈeθnɪk/ *adj.* 种族的;人种的

⑩ recollection /ˌrekəˈlekʃn/ *n.* 回忆;回忆起的事物

武夷山

Mount Wuyi

导入语 Lead-in

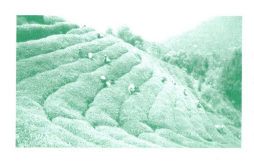

武夷山具有丰富的历史文化遗存：武夷架壑船棺是目前国内发现的年代最久远的悬棺，武夷宫是武夷山最古老的一座宫殿，武夷山还有堪称中国古书法艺术宝库的历代摩崖石刻，这里也是中国古代朱子理学的摇篮。大自然赐予了武夷山得天独厚的优越环境，吸引了历代文人墨客，为自然山水增添了无穷的魅力，武夷山也为湮灭的古文明和文化传统提供了独特的见证。1987年，武夷山被联合国教科文组织接纳为"人与生物圈"世界自然保护网成员；1992年，被联合国定为全球多样性保护区；1999年，被联合国教科文组织列入《世界遗产名录》，2017年被列入《世界自然与文化双重遗产名录》。

自然景观 第一部分

 ## 文化剪影 Cultural Outline

Mount Wuyi usually refers to the Little Mount Wuyi, which is located fifteen kilometers southwest of Wuyishan City, Fujian Province. It is known as "the first mountain in Fujian" and belongs to the typical Danxia landform. Mount Wuyi is a famous mountain of the three religions and a place where Confucian scholars **preached**① and taught. Wuyishan Nature Reserve is the best protected and most **diverse**② ecosystem on earth at the same **latitude**③. Mount Wuyi is a dual heritage of world culture and nature, a world biosphere reserve, a national key cultural relics protection unit, a national key scenic spot, a national 5A tourist attraction, a national nature reserve, a national water **conservancy**④ scenic area, a national **ecotourism**⑤ demonstration area, and a demonstration site of the national civilization scenic tourist area.

武夷山通常是指位于福建省武夷山市西南15千米的小武夷山，它也被称为"福建第一名山"，属于典型的丹霞地貌。武夷山是三教名山，也是儒家学者传道讲学的地方。武夷山自然保护区有着地球同纬度地区保护最好、物种最丰富的生态系统。武夷山是世界文化与自然双重遗产、世界生物圈保护区、全国重点文物保护单位、国家重点风景名胜区、国家5A级旅游景区、国家级自然保护区、国家水利风景区、国家生态旅游示范区和全国文明风景旅游区示范点。

Located in the heart of Mount Wuyi Scenic Area, Dahongpao

grows on the northern cliffs at the bottom of Jiulong Nest Valley. There are two **bonsai**⑥-style ancient tea gardens, one large and the other small. In 2007, the last 20 grams of Dahongpao Tea, collected from the three hundred and fifty-year-old mother tea tree, was treasured by the National Museum of China, and it was also the first time that modern tea was collected in the National Museum of China.

　　大红袍景区位于武夷山风景区的中心位置，大红袍生长在九龙窠谷底靠北面的悬崖峭壁上。这里有一大一小两个盆景式古茶园。2007年，最后一次采自350年母茶树的20克大红袍茶叶被中国国家博物馆珍藏，这也是现代茶叶第一次被藏入中国国家博物馆。

　　Mount Wuyi Nature Reserve is the largest nature reserve in Fujian Province and famous for its majestic mountains and **biodiversity**⑦. It is located in Mount Wuyi, Jianyang, Guangze of Fujian Province and Qianshan County of Jiangxi Province. The main peak, Mount Huanggang, located in Tongmu Village, Qianshan County, Jiangxi Province, is the highest peak in six provinces and one city in East China. It is known as the "Roof of East China" and the "Pillar of Wuyi".

　　武夷山自然保护区是福建省最大的自然保护区，以山貌雄伟和生物多样性而闻名，保护区位于福建省武夷山、建阳、光泽三市县和江西省铅山县处，主峰黄岗山位于江西省铅山县桐木村境内，是华东六省一市地区的最高峰，号称"华东屋脊"和"武夷支柱"。

佳句点睛　Punchlines

1. The beauty of Wuyi lies in the mountains, and the **spirituality**⑧ of Wuyi consists in the water.

武夷的美感在于山,武夷的灵性在于水。

2. Wuyi Mountain is known as "blue water and red mountain" and "strangeness and loveliness being the best in the Southeast".

武夷山素有"碧水丹山"和"奇秀甲东南"的美誉。

3. Wuyi Rock Tea, which is rich in Wuyi Mountain, has the function of "both medicine and drink".

武夷山盛产的武夷岩茶具有"药饮兼具"的功效。

 情景对话　Situational Dialogue

A: Do you know where Mount Wuyi is?

B: Of course. My hometown is right in Mount Wuyi. Mount Wuyi Scenic Spot is located in Wuyishan City, northwest of Fujian Province. Here is a typical Danxia landform with blue water and red mountain, famous for its "strangeness and loveliness being the best in the Southeast".

A: Are there any places worth visiting?

风景名胜

B: There're thirty-six peaks, seventy-two caves, ninety-nine rocks and one hundred and eight scenic spots. It has the wonder of Yellow Mountain, the loveliness of Guilin, the grandeur of Mount Tai, the **precipitousness**① of Mount Hua and the beauty of the West Lake. The essence of the Mount Wuyi landscape is at Jiuqu Creek. There are even stranger sights here.

A: Just tell me about them.

B: There're a series of mysterious hanging coffins on the cliff of Jiuqu Creek, which is a unique spectacle.

A: Oh, really? I'd like to see them for myself.

B: Mount Wuyi is also a famous historical and cultural mountain. Zhu Xi, a Confucian scholar of the Southern Song Dynasty, had lived here for more than forty years, writing books and preaching, making it a center of southeast culture. And the literati of all dynasties wrote more than two thousand beautiful poems here.

A: When you put it like that, Mount Wuyi is really a place to explore ancient wonders and visit scenic beauty.

B: You hit the nail on the head.

A: 你知道武夷山在哪里吗?

B: 当然知道。我的老家就在武夷山。武夷山风景名胜区位于福建省西北部武夷山市境内,这里是典型的丹霞地貌,碧水丹峰,被誉为"奇秀甲东南"。

A: 那里有什么值得参观的地方吗?

B: 景区内有三十六峰、七十二洞、九十九岩和一百零八景点。它有黄山之奇、桂林之秀、泰山之雄、华山之险和西湖之美。武夷山风景的精华在九曲溪。这里还有更奇特的景观呢。

A: 快给我讲讲。

B: 九曲溪边的悬崖峭壁上有一排排神秘的悬棺,这可是绝无仅有的奇观。

A: 噢,是吗？这我倒要去亲眼看看。

B: 武夷山还是一座历史文化名山呢。南宋理学家朱熹曾经在这里居住了四十多年,著书立说,传道授业,使这里成为东南文化的中心。历代文人雅士在此写下了两千多篇赞美诗文。

A: 听你这么一说,武夷山真不失为探奇访古和寻幽览胜之地。

B: 这你算说到了点子上。

生词注解　Notes

① preach /priːtʃ/　vt. 说教；讲道

② diverse /daɪˈvɜːs/　adj. 多种多样的；形形色色的

③ latitude /ˈlætɪtjuːd/　n. 纬度

④ conservancy /kənˈsɜːvənsɪ/　n. 保护；保存

⑤ ecotourism /ˈiːkəʊtʊərɪzəm/　n. 生态旅游

⑥ bonsai /ˈbɒnsaɪ/　n. 盆景；盆景艺术

⑦ biodiversity /ˌbaɪəʊdaɪˈvɜːsətɪ/　n. 生物多样性

⑧ spirituality /ˌspɪrɪtʃuˈælətɪ/　n. 灵性；精神性

⑨ precipitousness /prɪˈsɪpɪtəsnəs/　n. 险峻；山势高而陡峻

梵净山

Mount Fanjing

导入语 Lead-in

武陵山脉主峰梵净山是西南地区历史悠久的佛教名山,历来是当地人崇拜的神山和圣山。梵净山正式载入史册,始于汉代。到了宋代,佛教已经传入梵净山。北宋初年建立的西岩寺是贵州境内具有千年历史的著名古寺,也是梵净山佛教的祖庭。梵净山的闻名和开发均源自佛教,遍及梵净山区的寺庙群奠定了梵净山作为古佛道场的佛教地位,梵净山是中国五大佛教名山中唯一的弥勒菩萨道场,佛教文化也为梵净山披上了一层神秘的面纱。

文化剪影 Cultural Outline

Mount Fanjing, located at the **junction**① of Yinjiang County, Jiangkou County and Songtao County in the northeast of Guizhou Province, is the main peak of Wuling Mountains, the first famous mountain in Guizhou and the first peak in Wuling. Mount Fanjing is a national nature reserve. In 1982, it was listed as a world-class **ecological**② reserve by the United Nations. It is a member of the "Man and Biosphere Reserve Network" of the United Nations. Mount Fanjing is rich in wildlife resources, such as the Guizhou golden snub-nosed monkeys, dove trees and other rare species. The ancient geological structure of Mount Fanjing makes up its magnificent mountain landscape with thousands of **postures**③.

梵净山位于贵州省东北部的印江县、江口县、松桃县三县交界处,是武陵山脉主峰、贵州第一名山和武陵第一峰。梵净山是国家级自然保护区,1982年被联合国列为一级世界生态保护区,属于联合国"人与生物圈保护区网"成员。梵净山拥有丰富的野生动植物资源,如黔金丝猴、珙桐等珍稀物种。梵净山古老的地质结构构成了它姿态万千、雄奇壮丽的山地景观。

Mount Fanjing **Tribute**① Tea, which originated from "Tuanlong Tribute Tea", is made of tea leaves from 1,300～1,500 meters above sea level in Tuanlong Village at the western foot of Mount Fanjing and has a history of 500~600 years. It is bright in color, fluffy, high in amino acid, protein and tannic acid, rich in essential trace elements such as selenium and zinc and in nutrition, with a long-lasting fragrance and the functions of heat-clearing, **detoxification**⑤ and so on.

梵净山贡茶源于"团龙贡茶",就是以梵净山西麓团龙村海拔1300~1500米的茶叶为原料,采用独特的技术制成,至今已有五六百年历史。梵净山贡茶色泽亮、茸毛多,氨基酸、蛋白质和宁酸含量高,富含人体必需的硒、锌等微量元素,营养丰富,清香持久,具有清热、解毒等功效。

There's neither hot summer nor cold winter on Mount Fanjing. The air is not dry and there is no sand all the year round. The 10,000-meter sleeping Buddha lies on his back at the top of Mount Fanjing. For thousands of years, local people around Mount Fanjing worship it as the great Buddha; the mount is a Buddha and Buddha is a mount.

梵净山既无酷暑,也无寒冬,空气不干不燥,一年到头没有风沙。万米睡佛仰卧在梵净山顶。千百年来,当地百姓把梵净山当成大佛朝拜,山即一座佛,佛即一座山。

佳句点睛 Punchlines

1. As a marvelous creation **excelling**⑥ nature, the Golden Dome of Mount Fanjing is like a jade dragon howling straight into the sky, or like a huge bamboo shooting through the earth.

梵净山的金顶如玉龙啸天,直指苍穹,又像巨笋出土,巧夺天工。

2. The highest peak of Mount Fanjing — Mount Phoenix, located in the south of the dome, is named for the shape of the mountain like a phoenix spreading its wings and holding high its head.

梵净山的最高峰凤凰山位于穹隆之南,因山形如一只展翅昂头的凤凰而得名。

3. The red-cloud gold top resembles the Buddha's two fingers, or the **totem**[7] of life, therefore it is also called "The First Peak in the World".

红云金顶似佛手二指禅,又如生命的图腾,因此又被称为"天下第一峰"。

情景对话　Situational Dialogue

A: Have you ever been to Mount Fanjing?

B: I went there once last summer.

A: How's it going over there?

B: It can be said without **exaggeration**[8] that it is an oasis of life.

A: What do you mean?

B: Many rare plants and animals specially protected by the state are resting there in freedom and peace. As early as 1986, it was listed as a national nature reserve.

风景名胜

A: Then, why is it called Mount Fanjing?

B: It is not only the highest mountain in Guizhou, but also one of the five famous Buddhist mountains in China. Mount Fanjing itself has a strong color of Buddhism, deriving from "The **Brahma**① Pure Land" of Buddhism.

A: Oh, I see. And what else are there?

B: It can be said that it is a combination of being "primitive" "ancient" "profound" and "magical". This is also the **habitat**② of the golden snub-nosed monkey. There're currently four types of golden snub-nosed monkeys found in China. The number of golden snub-nosed monkeys in Guizhou is the rarest, with only about 700 remaining, so it is called "The Only Child in the World".

A: I've also heard that the weather at the top of Mount Fanjing varies from minute to minute. Is that true?

B: Yes, it is. This is the very magic of Mount Fanjing.

A: 你去过梵净山吗?

B: 去年夏天去过一次。

A: 那里怎么样啊?

B: 毫不夸张地说,那里是一片生命的绿洲。

A: 此话怎讲?

B: 好多国家重点保护的珍稀动植物都在那里自由和平地休养生息。早在1986年,它就被列为国家级自然保护区了。

A: 它为什么叫梵净山呢?

B: 梵净山不仅是贵州第一高山,也是中国五大佛教名山之一,梵净山本身就具有浓厚的佛教色彩,它得名于佛教中的"梵天净土"。

A: 噢,我明白了。它还有什么特色?

B: 梵净山可以说是集"原始""古老""深厚"和"神奇"于一身。这里还是黔金丝猴的栖息地。我国目前共发现了四种金丝猴,黔金丝猴的数量最为稀少,仅存七百只左右,因此被称为"世界独生子"。

A: 我还听说梵净山的山顶气象瞬息万变。是真的吗?

B: 是真的。这也正是梵净山的神奇之处。

生词注解　Notes

① junction /ˈdʒʌŋkʃn/　*n.* 交叉点;接合点

② ecological /iːkəˈlɒdʒɪkl/　*adj.* 生态的;生态学的

③ posture /ˈpɒstʃə(r)/　*n.* (坐立的)姿势;立场

④ tribute /ˈtrɪbjuːt/　*n.* 贡物;颂词

⑤ detoxification /diːˌtɒksɪfɪˈkeɪʃn/　*n.* 解毒;解毒作用

⑥ excel /ɪkˈsel/　*vt.* 胜过;擅长

⑦ totem /ˈtəʊtəm/　*n.* 图腾;崇拜物

⑧ exaggeration /ɪɡˌzædʒəˈreɪʃn/　*n.* 夸张;夸大之词

⑨ Brahma /ˈbrɑːmə/　*n.* 梵天(印度教主神)

⑩ habitat /ˈhæbɪtæt/　*n.* 栖息地;产地

中国丹霞地貌

Danxia Landform in China

导入语 Lead-in

丹霞地貌既像"玫瑰色的云彩",又像"深红色的霞光"。丹霞是一种形成于西太平洋活性大陆边缘断陷盆地极厚沉积物上的地貌景观,主要由红色砂岩和砾岩组成,反映的是在干热气候条件下氧化陆相湖盆沉积的环境。2010年,中国丹霞被正式列入《世界自然遗产名录》。中国丹霞地貌与涉及丹霞地貌的世界文化遗产地相比,具有更突出的丹霞地貌科学价值和美学价值,以及良好的生态环境价值,以丹霞为载体形成的丹霞文化更注重天人和谐之美。

自 然 景 观　第一部分

文化剪影　Cultural Outline

　　Danxia in China includes the natural Danxia red basin landscape of Mount Langshan in Hunan, which is known as "the soul of Danxia and the treasure of the country", Mount Danxia in Guangdong, Mount Longhu in Jiangxi and Mount Jianglang in Zhejiang, as well as Chishui Danxia in Guizhou at the junction of Sichuan Basin and Yunnan-Guizhou Plateau, China's largest **distribution**[①] area of Danxia.

　　中国丹霞地貌包括被誉为"丹霞之魂和国之瑰宝"的湖南崀山天然丹霞红盆地貌、广东丹霞山、江西龙虎山和浙江江郎山，以及位于四川盆地和云贵高原结合部的中国最大丹霞地貌分布区——贵州赤水丹霞等。

　　Mount Jianglang is known as "the first peak of Danxia in China". There are rock caves and **cloud-cascades**[②] as well as extreme strangeness and precipitousness. The mountains are verdant, overflowing with clouds and mist and with beautiful sunglow. It can be said that the sky and the mount are of the same color, the clouds and the peak combining together.

　　江郎山被誉为"神州丹霞第一峰"，其岩洞云瀑奇险陡峻，群山苍翠，云雾弥漫其间，霞光旖旎，天山一色，云峰一体。

　　There are waterfalls, wetlands, **lush**[③] forest and other natural beauty in Chishui Danxia, with forest coverage rate of more than 90%. The most unique characteristics of Chishui Danxia is a large area of ancient vegetation, more than 2,000 species of plants and animals as well as rare and endangered plants and animals. The Danxia landform in Chishui is formed an interesting contrast by Danxia red cliffs, lonely peaks and narrow ridges, strange mountains and stones, rock corridors and caves, Danxia gorges, green forests, and flying waterfalls and flowing springs.

赤水丹霞有瀑布、湿地、翠林等自然美景,森林覆盖率超过90%。大面积古植被、两千余种动植物和珍稀濒危动植物是赤水丹霞最独有的特征。丹霞赤壁、孤峰窄脊、奇山异石、岩廊洞穴、丹霞峡谷、绿色森林、飞瀑流泉更是与赤水丹霞地貌相映成趣。

 佳句点睛 Punchlines

1. Danxia refers to the isolated peaks and steep strange rocks formed by long-term weathering and **erosion**① of red sandstone.

丹霞是指红色砂砾岩经长期风化剥离和流水侵蚀形成的孤立山峰和奇岩怪石。

2. The best of Danxia landform is the window-lattice-style and palace-style Danxia landforms.

窗棂式丹霞地貌和宫殿式丹霞地貌是丹霞地貌中的精品。

3. Colorful Danxia wonders are amazed for **staggered**⑤ beddings, steep rock walls, great **momentum**⑥, strange shapes and multicolor.

七彩丹霞奇观因层理交错、岩壁陡峭、气势磅礴、造型奇特和色彩斑斓而称奇。

情景对话　Situational Dialogue

A: Is China Danxia a place?

B: No, it's a geological term.

A: Do you mean there're Danxia in many parts of China?

B: Yes.

A: Why is it called Danxia, then?

B: Because the Danxia landform is like "rosy clouds" or "crimson sunglow".

A: Oh, I see. Do you know where Danxia is the most famous?

B: As far as I know, the most famous is Mount Danxia in Renhua County, Guangdong Province. The whole mountain is coated with red sandstones; overlooking the whole mountain, you'll see the color is red like lilium **concolor**⑦ and bright like sunglow, also known as "Red Stone Garden".

A: What's the most **distinctive**⑧?

B: Brocade⑨ Rock is both the earliest and the most attractive part of Mount Danxia, formed by four caves in front and back, which are **spectacular**⑩ and beautiful.

A: It's got to be more than these?

B: Of course. I've heard that there are twelve old sceneries and twelve new ones on Mount Danxia, and there's a lot to see there.

A: 中国丹霞是一个地方吗?

B: 不是,这是一个地质总称。

A: 你是说,中国好多地方都有丹霞吗?

B: 是的。

A: 为什么叫丹霞呢?

B: 因为丹霞地貌既像"玫瑰色的云彩",又像"深红色的霞光"。

A: 噢,我明白了。你知道哪里的丹霞最有名吗?

B: 据我所知,广东省仁化县境内的丹霞山最有名,整座山遍布红色砂砾岩,远眺全山,色如渥丹,灿若明霞,这里又被称为"红石花园"。

A: 最有特色的丹霞在哪里?

B: 锦石岩,这里既是丹霞山开发最早的地方,也是最吸引人的所在。锦石岩由前后四个岩洞连成一体,蔚为壮观,美不胜收。

A: 应该不止这些吧?

B: 当然不止,我听说丹霞山有古十二景和新十二景,那里好看的地方多着呢。

生词注解 Notes

① distribution /ˌdɪstrɪˈbjuːʃn/ *n.* 分布;分配

自然景观 第一部分

② cascade /kæˈskeɪd/ *n.* 小瀑布；瀑布状物

③ lush /lʌʃ/ *adj.* 郁郁葱葱的；苍翠繁茂的

④ erosion /ɪˈrəʊʒn/ *n.* 侵蚀；腐蚀

⑤ staggered /ˈstæɡəd/ *adj.* 错列的；震惊的

⑥ momentum /məˈmentəm/ *n.* 冲力；动力

⑦ lilium concolor /ˈlɪliəm kɒnˈkʌlə(r)/ *n.* 渥丹；山丹

⑧ distinctive /dɪˈstɪŋktɪv/ *adj.* 独特的；有特色的

⑨ brocade /brəˈkeɪd/ *n.* 织锦；锦缎

⑩ spectacular /spekˈtækjələ(r)/ *adj.* 壮观的；引人入胜的

风景名胜

中国南方喀斯特

South China Karst

  导入语 Lead-in

喀斯特是水对可溶性岩石溶蚀形成的地表和地下形态的总称,按气候带分为热带喀斯特、亚热带喀斯特、温带喀斯特、寒带喀斯特和干旱区喀斯特五种;按岩性分为石灰岩喀斯特、白云岩喀斯特、石膏喀斯特和盐喀斯特四种。中国南方喀斯特拥有最显著的塔状、锥状喀斯特地貌类型和立体喀斯特景观,是世界上最壮观的热带至亚热带喀斯特地貌样本之一,也是重要的世界自然遗产,主要由重庆武隆喀斯特、贵州荔波喀斯特和云南石林喀斯特组成。2007年,中国南方喀斯特被联合国教科文组织列入《世界自然遗产名录》。

文化剪影　Cultural Outline

　　The karst landforms in China are widely **distributed**①. The karst landforms in the south cover 50,000 square kilometers, mainly in Yunnan, Guizhou, Guangxi and Chongqing. The karst area in the south covers 55％ of the entire karst area in China, composed of karst landforms in Shilin of Yunnan, Libo of Guizhou, Wulong of Chongqing, Guilin of Guangxi, Shibing of Guizhou, Jinfoshan of Chongqing and Huanjiang of Guangxi.

　　中国喀斯特地貌分布广泛。位于南方地区的喀斯特地貌覆盖了5万平方千米，主要分布于云南、贵州、广西、重庆等省区，由云南石林、贵州荔波、重庆武隆、广西桂林、贵州施秉、重庆金佛山和广西环江的喀斯特地貌组成，占整个中国喀斯特面积的55％。

　　The Stone Forest was formed 270 million years ago. After a long geological evolution and changes in the complex **paleogeographic**② environment, the current extremely precious geological relics have been formed. It covers many types of karst landforms on earth. Almost all stone forests distributed around the world are gathered here. Stone teeth, peak clusters, karst hills, karst caves, karst lakes, waterfalls, and underground rivers are scattered all over the place. It is a typical plateau karst **ecosystem**③ and the richest stereoscopic **panorama**④.

风景名胜

石林形成于2.7亿年前,经过漫长的地质演化和复杂的古地理环境变迁,形成了当前极其珍贵的地质遗迹。它涵盖了地球上众多的喀斯特地貌类型,分布于世界各地的石林几乎都汇集于此,石牙、峰丛、溶丘、溶洞、溶蚀湖、瀑布和地下河错落有致,是典型的高原喀斯特生态系统和最丰富的立体全景图。

The diverse karst landforms show the features of karst landforms from the humid tropics to the subtropical zone. It consists of the sword-shaped, columnar and pagoda-shaped karst of the Stone Forest of Yunnan, the forest karst of Libo County, Guizhou, and the three-dimensional karst of Wulong, Chongqing.

多样性喀斯特地形展示了由多湿的热带至亚热带的喀斯特地貌特征,包括云南石林的剑状、柱状、塔状喀斯特,以及贵州荔波的森林喀斯特和重庆武隆的立体喀斯特。

佳句点睛　Punchlines

1. Libo's karst virgin forest, water forest and **funnel**① forest are collectively called "Libo's Three Wonders".
   荔波喀斯特原始森林、水上森林和漏斗森林,合称"荔波三绝"。

2. The Stone Forest is **dominated**② by karst landscapes, well known for its "majesty, strangeness, perilousness, loveliness, quietude, mystery and vastness".

石林以喀斯特景观为主,以"雄、奇、险、秀、幽、奥、旷"著称。

3. Qinglong (Green Dragon) Bridge is a bridge with the largest vertical height difference of three natural bridges in Wulong. When the sun sets, myriads of evening rays are shining in all directions, flickering now and then, as if a real dragon flying to the azure sky.

青龙桥是武隆天生三桥中垂直高差最大的一座天生桥,夕阳西下,霞光万道,忽明忽暗,似一条真龙直上青天。

情景对话　Situational Dialogue

A: Do you know where "The First Cave in the World" is?

B: You mean Furong Cave? It's in Wulong, Chongqing. It can be called the "Cave Science Museum".

A: Why did you say that?

B: Because of its gigantic scale, rich and diverse **sediments**⑦, numerous **dissolution**⑧ forms, and the inexhaustible **stalactites**⑨, which really record its long historical evolution.

A: I've heard that there's the world's largest natural bridge group.

B: Exactly. It is the world's largest beaded natural bridge group. All the three karst natural bridges are above the same **canyon**⑩.

A: Which three are all?

B: Tianlong (Heavenly Dragon) Bridge, Qinglong (Green Dragon) Bridge and Heilong (Black Dragon) Bridge. The three natural bridges rank first in the world in total height, arch height and deck thickness.

A: I'll surely go there and experience the magic of nature.

B: OK, let's go together till then.

A: 你知道"天下第一洞"在哪里吗？

B: 你是说芙蓉洞吧？在重庆武隆。芙蓉洞堪称"洞穴科学博物馆"。

A: 何出此言？

B: 因为芙蓉洞洞体规模宏大，洞内沉积物丰富多样，洞穴溶蚀形态万千，钟乳石应接不暇，这些都真实记录了它漫长的历史演进过程。

A: 听说那里还有世界上最大的天生桥群？

B: 没错，那是世界上规模最大的串珠式天生桥群。三座喀斯特天生桥都在同一峡谷之上。

A: 都是哪三座？

B: 天龙桥、青龙桥和黑龙桥。这三座天生桥总高度、桥拱高度和桥面厚度都位居世界第一。

A: 我一定要到那里去亲自感受一下大自然的鬼斧神工。

B: 好啊，到时候咱们一起去。

生词注解　Notes

① distribute /dɪˈstrɪbjuːt/　*vt.* 分布；分配

② paleogeographic /ˌpæliˈɒgrəfik/ *adj.* 古地理的

③ ecosystem /ˈiːkəʊsɪstəm/ *n.* 生态系统

④ panorama /ˌpænəˈrɑːmə/ *n.* 全景图

⑤ funnel /ˈfʌnl/ *n.* 漏斗；漏斗状物

⑥ dominate /ˈdɒmɪneɪt/ *vt.* 支配；占优势

⑦ sediment /ˈsedɪmənt/ *n.* 沉积；沉淀物

⑧ dissolution /ˌdɪsəˈluːʃn/ *n.* 分解；溶解

⑨ stalactite /ˈstæləktaɪt/ *n.* 钟乳石

⑩ canyon /ˈkænjən/ *n.* 峡谷；溪谷

风景名胜

黄龙寺-九寨沟风景名胜区

Huanglong Temple and Jiuzhai Valley Scenic and Historic Interest Area

 导入语 Lead-in

　　黄龙寺风景区位于四川省阿坝藏族羌族自治州松潘县境内，是中国唯一保护完好的高原湿地，与九寨沟相距100千米，地貌特征是山雄峡峻。沟中有许多彩池，随着周围景色和阳光照射角度的变化而变幻出五彩的颜色，因此被誉为"人间瑶池"。黄龙寺与九寨沟同时被联合国教科文组织列入《世界文化与自然遗产名录》。黄龙寺-九寨沟风景名胜区是世界自然遗产、世界人与生物圈保护区、国家5A级旅游景区和国家重点风景名胜区。

自然景观 第一部分

 文化剪影 Cultural Outline

Huanglong Temple Scenic Area is located in the southern part of the Minshan Mountains in Songpan County, Aba Tibetan and Qiang Autonomous **Prefecture**① in northern Sichuan Province. It belongs to the transition zone from the eastern edge of the Qinghai-Tibet Plateau to the Sichuan Basin. The highest peak, Xuebao Peak, the main peak of the Minshan Mountains, is 5,588 meters above sea level and is covered with snow all year round. It is the easternmost point where modern **glaciers**② exist in China. Jiuzhaigou, located in Jiuzhaigou County, Sichuan Province, in the **alpine**③ gorge at the junction of Songpan and Pingwu, is a valley of more than 40 kilometers deep in the Minshan Mountains, named after nine Tibetan villages around it.

黄龙寺风景区位于四川省北部阿坝藏族羌族自治州松潘县境内的岷山山脉南段，属青藏高原东部边缘向四川盆地的过渡地带，最高峰岷山主峰雪宝顶海拔5588米，终年积雪，是中国现存冰川的最东点。九寨沟位于四川省九寨沟县境内，地处松潘、平武交界处的高山峡谷之中，系岷山山脉一条纵深40多千米的山沟谷地，因周围有九个藏族村寨而得名。

Jiuzhai Valley is composed of a main **gully**④ and six branch gullies. There are hundreds of ladder-shaped colored lakes and countless flying waterfalls and flowing springs in the gullies, where the scenery is beautiful and wonderful, rare in the world, and enjoys the reputation of "fairytale world". The virgin forest is more than two hundred square kilometers, and there are dozens of rare animals such as giant pandas, golden snub-nosed monkeys, red pandas and **takins**⑤.

九寨沟由主沟和六条支沟组成,沟内有数百个阶梯状的彩色湖泊,无数飞瀑流泉奔泻,景色秀丽奇绝,世所罕见,有"童话世界"之誉。原始森林达两百多平方千米,珍稀动物有大熊猫、金丝猴、小熊猫、扭角羚等几十种。

Huanglong Temple Scenic Area gathers colorful ponds, snow mountains, canyons, forests, beaches, ancient temples and folklore in one. Huanglong Valley, the main scenic spot, is located under the top of Xuebao, the main peak of Minshan Mountain, facing the source of the Minjiang River like a dragon, honored as the "Chinese Symbol". Huanglong Temple Scenic Area is famous in the world for its grand, **ingenious**⑥ and rich surface landscape and its rare karst landform, known as "The Fairyland on Earth".

黄龙寺风景区集彩池、雪山、峡谷、森林、滩流、古寺和民俗于一体。主景区黄龙沟位于岷山主峰雪宝顶下,面临涪江源流,蜿蜒似龙,被誉为"中华象征"。黄龙寺风景区以宏大、奇巧和丰富的地表景观为主,以罕见的岩溶地貌驰名世界,被称为"人间仙境"。

佳句点睛 Punchlines

1. According to the legend, when Yu of Xia combated the flood, he got to Maozhou, and a yellow dragon carried the boat to guide the water for him. Later generations built the temple to worship it, so Huanglong (Yellow Dragon) Temple got its name.

传说夏禹治水至茂州,有黄龙为其负舟导水,后人建庙以祀,黄龙寺因而得名。

2. The scenic area is composed of Huanglong Temple, Mouni Gully, Xueshan Ridge, Xuebao Summit and Danyun Gorge and so on.

景区由黄龙寺、牟尼沟、雪山梁、雪宝顶和丹云峡等景点组成。

3. Color Pool is different in depth and size, bright as pearls, presenting a crystal, smooth, beautiful and colorful scenery.

彩池深浅不一,大小悬殊,明亮如珠,呈现出晶莹润泽、美丽多彩的景色。

 情景对话 Situational Dialogue

A: Do you know the origin of Jiuzhai Valley?

B: Yes. It's named after nine Tibetan villages in the gully.

A: What is the most peculiar in Jiuzhai Valley?

风景名胜

B: It's characterized by the most amazing waterscape, with springs, waterfalls, rivers, and beaches connected together to form a beautiful view of "water flowing between the trees and trees growing in the water".

A: What is the connection between Huanglong Temple Scenic Area and Jiuzhai Valley?

B: The distance between them is 100 kilometers.

A: This is a bit **far-fetched**①.

B: Huanglong Temple and Jiuzhai Valley were included in *The World Cultural and Natural Heritage List* by UNESCO at the same time.

A: Oh, that's it. What are the characteristics of Huanglong Temple Scenic Area?

B: It is the only well-preserved plateau wetland in China, known as the "Yaochi (**abode**② of **immortals**③) on earth."

A: 你知道九寨沟的由来吗?

B: 知道。它因沟内有九个藏族村寨而得名。

A: 九寨沟最奇特的是什么?

B: 它以水景最为奇丽,泉、瀑、河、滩连成一体,形成了"水在树间流,树在水中长"的美景。

A: 黄龙寺风景区跟九寨沟有什么联系?

B: 黄龙寺风景区与九寨沟相距100千米。

A: 这有些牵强吧。

B: 黄龙寺与九寨沟同时被联合国教科文组织列入《世界文化与自然遗产名录》。

A: 噢,是这样。那黄龙寺风景区有什么特色?

B: 它是中国唯一保护完好的高原湿地,被誉为"人间瑶池"。

生词注解 Notes

① prefecture /ˈpriːfektʃə(r)/ *n.* 辖区;太守

② glacier /ˈglæsɪə(r)/ *n.* 冰河;冰川

③ alpine /ˈælpaɪn/ *adj.* 高山的

④ gully /ˈgʌlɪ/ *n.* 冲沟;陡峭的岩沟

⑤ takin /ˈtɑːkɪn/ *n.* 扭角羚;羚牛

⑥ ingenious /ɪnˈdʒiːnɪəs/ *adj.* 灵巧的;新颖的

⑦ far-fetched /ˌfɑːˈfetʃt/ *adj.* 牵强附会的

⑧ abode /əˈbəʊd/ *n.* 住所;住宅

⑨ immortal /ɪˈmɔːtl/ *n.* 神仙;不朽人物

风景名胜

四川大熊猫栖息地

Sichuan Giant Panda Habitats

 导入语　Lead-in

四川大熊猫栖息地由世界上第一只大熊猫的发现地宝兴县，及中国四川省境内的卧龙自然保护区等七处自然保护区和青城山-都江堰风景名胜区等九处风景名胜区组成。大熊猫分布于陕西秦岭、四川、甘肃交界的岷山地区、邛崃山系、大相岭、小相岭和凉山山系。这些地区目前保存了世界上30%以上的野生大熊猫，是全球最大、最完整的大熊猫栖息地。四川大熊猫栖息地已被选定为全球25个生物多样性热点地区之一，同时被世界自然基金会（WWF）确定为全球200个生态区之一。

文化剪影 Cultural Outline

Sichuan Giant Panda **habitats**① include Wolong, Mount Siguniang and the Jiajin Mountains, covering Chengdu, Aba, Ya'an, and Garze. More than 30% of the world's wild pandas live here. It is the largest and most complete panda habitat in the world.

四川大熊猫栖息地包括卧龙、四姑娘山、夹金山脉,涵盖成都、阿坝、雅安和甘孜。这里生活着世界上30%以上的野生大熊猫,是全球最大、最完整的大熊猫栖息地。

Mount Siguniang belongs to the Qionglai Mountains, where Mount Yaomei, the main peak, is 6,240 meters above sea level. Mount Siguniang is made up of four **adjoining**② snow peaks, clad in silvery white all year round, like four beautiful fairies in white, hence it got the name. Mount Siguniang is composed of three gullies such as Changping Gully, Shuangqiao Gully and Haizi Gully.

四姑娘山属邛崃山脉,主峰幺妹峰海拔6240米。四姑娘山由四座毗连的雪峰组成,终年银装素裹,如四位美丽的白衣仙女,因而得名。四姑娘山由三条沟组成,分别为长坪沟、双桥沟和海子沟。

There're about 240 wild giant pandas in the Jiajin Mountains, **accounting for**③ about a quarter of the total in Sichuan and a quarter of the national total. Since 1955, the Jiajin Mountains region of Ya'an

City has provided living giant pandas to the country, and is the largest supplier of wild giant pandas in the world. The habitat of giant pandas in the Jiajin Mountains is also the type specimen of 82 species of **vertebrates**① such as giant pandas, golden snub-nosed monkeys and 105 types of higher plants such as dove trees.

夹金山脉现有野生大熊猫约240只,约占四川总数的四分之一和全国总数的四分之一。雅安市夹金山脉地区自1955年起向国家提供活体大熊猫,是国际上最大的野生大熊猫供给地。夹金山脉大熊猫栖息地还是大熊猫、金丝猴等82种脊椎动物与珙桐等105种高等植物的模式标本产地。

佳句点睛　Punchlines

1. Surrounded by mountains, Wolong Nature Reserve is a natural paradise for giant pandas, with **uninterrupted**⑤ peaks and tall trees and lush grass.

卧龙自然保护区群山环抱,奇峰连绵,林高草茂,是大熊猫的天然乐园。

2. Except the ears, eyes, mouth and limbs are black, the other parts of the giant panda are white, which is really black and white sharply contrasted.

大熊猫除了耳朵、眼睛、嘴巴和四肢是黑色外,其他部位都呈白色,真是黑白分明。

3. There is a bamboo forest on the green grass. Giant pandas particularly like to eat bamboo leaves and shoots.

绿茵茵的草地上长着一片竹林，大熊猫特别喜欢吃竹叶和竹笋。

情景对话　Situational Dialogue

A: Do you know what giant pandas usually eat?

B: They mainly eat bamboos.

A: How do they eat?

B: The **staple**① of giant pandas in different mountain ranges is also different, and their recipes will change with the change of mountain chains and seasons. They like to eat different kinds of bamboo shoots in spring and summer. They mostly eat bamboo leaves in autumn and bamboo poles in winter.

A: Why do they eat bamboos instead of meat, then?

B: This is related to changes in their living environment. After the **glacier**② attack, giant pandas could only survive by gradually changing their diet. In the process of long-term adaptation to the environment, they have changed from eating meat to bamboos.

A: Oh, that's what happened. So what are they particular about?

B: They like cold-arrow bamboos, ink bamboos and water bamboos, especially bamboo shoots.

A: Do they eat a lot?

B: Yes, they eat a lot. They eat 20 kilograms of tender bamboos

风景名胜

every day and absorb **nutrients**⑧ from a lot of fiber. Because they need to digest a lot of fiber and **lignin**⑨, especially like to drink water.

A: What does a giant panda's life usually look like?

B: In addition to eating, they just sleep, wake up and start eating again. What really a life of ease, leisure and carefreeness!

A：你知道大熊猫平时都吃什么？

B：它们主要吃竹子。

A：它们是怎么吃的呢？

B：不同山系的大熊猫主食竹类也不同，它们的食谱会随着山系和季节的变化而变化。春夏季，大熊猫最爱吃不同种类的竹笋，秋季多以竹叶为主食，冬季则以竹竿为主食。

A：那大熊猫为什么吃竹子而不吃肉呢？

B：这跟它们的生活环境变化有关，冰川袭击之后，大熊猫只有逐渐改变食性才能生存下去。在长期适应环境的过程中，它们从食肉变为食竹。

A：噢，原来是这么回事。它们还有什么特别之处？

B：它们爱吃冷箭竹、墨竹、水竹，尤其是爱吃竹笋。

A：它们的食量大吗？

B：大得很，它们每天要吃20千克的嫩竹，从大量纤维中吸收营养，因为每天要消化大量纤维和木质素，所以大熊猫特爱喝水。

A：大熊猫平时的生活是什么样子？

B：它们除了吃就是睡，睡醒了又开始吃。真是优哉游哉，逍遥自在。

生词注解　Notes

① habitat /ˈhæbɪtæt/　n. 栖息地；产地

② adjoining /əˈdʒɔɪnɪŋ/　adj. 邻接的；毗连的

③ account /əˈkaʊnt/ for　（比例）占

④ vertebrate /ˈvɜːtɪbrət/　n. 脊椎动物

⑤ uninterrupted /ˌʌnˌɪntəˈrʌptɪd/　adj. 不间断的；连续的

⑥ staple /ˈsteɪpl/　n. 主食；主题

⑦ glacier /ˈɡlæsɪə(r)/　n. 冰河；冰川

⑧ nutrient /ˈnjuːtriənt/　n. 营养物；滋养物

⑨ lignin /ˈlɪɡnɪn/　n. 木质素；木质

云南三江并流保护区

Three Parallel Rivers Protected Region in Yunnan

导入语 Lead-in

云南三江并流保护区是世界上罕见的多民族、多语言、多种习俗并存的聚居地,是中国生物多样性最丰富的区域,也是世界上温带生物多样性最丰富的区域。"三江"指金沙江、澜沧江和怒江。石鼓镇是茶马古道的要塞和南下大理、北进藏区的交通枢纽,是金沙江上游的一座历史文化重镇。1977年,镇上建立了红军渡江纪念碑。1997年,石鼓镇被列为爱国主义教育基地。1999年,镇上又修建了红军渡江雕塑。2003年,三江并流保护区作为世界自然遗产被联合国教科文组织列入《世界自然遗产名录》。

文化剪影 Cultural Outline

The Three **Parallel**① Rivers Natural Landscape is composed of Nujiang River, Lancang River, Jinsha River, and the mountains in the river basin. The entire area is located at the junction of the three major regions of East Asia, South Asia, and the Qinghai-Tibet Plateau. The Three Parallel Rivers **Conservation**② Region in Yunnan is located in the Three Rivers National Park in the northwestern mountainous area of Yunnan Province. It is a representative area of rare alpine landforms and its evolution in the world, and also one of the regions with the abundant biological species in the world. The special geological structure of the Three Parallel Rivers Region, the most concentrated biodiversity in Eurasia, rich human resources, and beautiful and magical natural landscapes make this region a unique world wonder.

三江并流自然景观由怒江、澜沧江、金沙江及其流域内的山脉组成，整个区域地处东亚、南亚和青藏高原三大区域的交汇处。云南三江并流保护区位于云南省西北山区的三江国家公园内，是世界上罕见的高山地貌及其演化的代表地区，也是世界上生物物种较为丰富的地区之一。三江并流地区特殊的地质构造、欧亚大陆最集中的生物多样性、丰富的人文资源、美丽神奇的自然景观，使该地区成为独一无二的世界奇观。

The Three Parallel Rivers is a history textbook on the evolution of the earth. The **collision**① of the Indian plate and the Eurasian plate led to the uplift of the Qinghai-Tibet Plateau, forming the same arrangement of Dulong River, Mount Gaoligong, Nujiang River, Lancang River, Yunling Ridge, and Jinsha River within 150 kilometers. The main body of the Hengduan Mountains is composed of huge mountains and large rivers, which is the unique natural landscape of **alpine**① and gorge in the world.

三江并流是一部地球演化的历史教科书，印度板块与欧亚板块的碰撞导致青藏高原隆起，在150千米内形成了排列整齐的独龙江、高黎贡山、怒江、澜沧江、云岭和金沙江。横断山脉的主体由大山和大江构成，这是世界上绝无仅有的高山峡谷自然景观。

The largest bay on the Yangtze River is next to Shigu Town. There is a Tiehong Bridge on the left side in Shigu Town. The Tiehong Bridge is used with a 17-meter-long iron chain as a beam, wooden planks on both sides, and iron chains on both sides as railings. Gatehouses are built on both ends of the bridge. Shigu Town has always been a major town for trading between the Tibetan and Han areas.

长江第一大湾在石鼓镇旁。石鼓镇镇左侧有铁虹桥，铁虹桥用17米长的铁链作梁，上铺木板，两边用铁链作栏杆，桥两头均建有门楼。石鼓镇历来是藏区与汉族地区交易的重镇。

佳句点睛　Punchlines

1. The Three Parallel Rivers Region is the most **abundant**⑤ geological and **geomorphological**⑥ museum in the world.

三江并流地区是世界上蕴藏最丰富的地质地貌博物馆。

2. In the Three Parallel Rivers Scenic Region, high mountains and snow peaks cross the mountain, and the **elevation**⑦ changes are distributed vertically.

三江并流景区内,高山雪峰横亘,海拔变化呈垂直分布。

3. Tiger-leaping Gorge is the first grand canyon on the Jinsha River, and it is also a world-famous grand canyon.

虎跳峡是金沙江上的第一大峡谷,更是全球著名的大峡谷。

情景对话　Situational Dialogue

A: What's your impression on the Yunnan's Three Parallel Rivers Protected Region?

B: My impression on it is very unique.

A: What is unique?

B: You know that the great mountain ranges in China are in the east-west direction, while the Hengduan Mountains here are in the north-south direction. In addition, the Nujiang River, the Lancang River, and the Jinsha River, which originated from the Qinghai-Tibet **Plateau**[⑧], crossed the Hengduan Mountains from north to south, each surging for hundreds of kilometers without **intersecting**[⑨] each other.

A: What about the species here?

B: 77 species of national protected animals such as rare and endangered Yunnan golden monkeys, **antelopes**[⑩], snow leopards, Bengal tigers, and black-necked cranes are inhabited here, where there're 34 species of national protected plants such as Taiwania and yew, and 22 ethnic groups including Naxi, Tibet and Lisu people. Shangri-La is here. This is still the world's biological gene bank.

A: It's special enough.

B: Do you wanna go?

A: Of course, I can't wait.

B: Then I will guide you and guarantee you a worthwhile trip.

A：你对云南三江并流保护区印象怎么样？

B：我认为它非常独特。

A：独特在什么地方？

B：你知道，中国的山脉都是东西走向，而这里的横断山脉却都是南北走向。另外，发源于青藏高原的怒江、澜沧江和金沙江从北到南穿过横断山脉，各自汹涌奔腾几百公里互不交汇。

A：这里的物种如何？

B：这里栖息着珍稀濒危的滇金丝猴、羚羊、雪豹、孟加拉虎、黑颈鹤等77种国家级保护动物,生长着秃杉、红豆杉等34种国家级保护植物,这里还生活着纳西族、藏族、傈僳族等22个民族。香格里拉就在这里,这里还是世界生物基因库呢。

A: 真够特别的。

B: 你想不想去?

A: 当然想,我都等不及了。

B: 那我给你当向导,保证你不虚此行。

生词注解　Notes

① parallel /ˈpærəlel/　*adj.* 平行的;类似的

② conservation /ˌkɒnsəˈveɪʃn/　*n.* 保护;保持

③ collision /kəˈlɪʒn/　*n.* 碰撞;冲突

④ alpine /ˈælpaɪn/　*adj.* 高山的

⑤ abundant /əˈbʌndənt/　*adj.* 盛产的;充裕的

⑥ geomorphological /dʒɪˌmɔrfəˈlɑdʒɪkl/　*adj.* 地貌的;地形的

⑦ elevation /ˌelɪˈveɪʃn/　*n.* 海拔;高地

⑧ plateau /ˈplætəʊ/　*n.* 高原

⑨ intersect /ˌɪntəˈsekt/　*v.* 相交;交叉

⑩ antelope /ˈæntɪləʊp/　*n.* 羚羊

风景名胜

红河哈尼梯田

Red River Hani Terraces

导入语 Lead-in

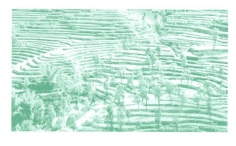

红河哈尼梯田位于云南省红河哈尼彝族自治州,是以哈尼族为主的各族人民利用当地"一山分四季,十里不同天"的独特地理环境创造的农耕文明奇观,已有1300多年的历史。这里的梯田规模宏大,绵延红河南岸的元阳、绿春、金平等县。这里水源充沛,空气湿润,云雾缭绕,变化多端,将山谷与梯田装点得既含蓄自然又生动有趣,令人耳目一新。2010年,红河哈尼梯田被联合国粮农组织评为"农业文化遗产保护单位"。2013年,红河哈尼梯田被联合国教科文组织列入《世界遗产名录》。

自然景观 第一部分

 文化剪影 Cultural Outline

Hani Terraces are magnificent and unique. The Hani people cultivate terraced fields, adapt to local conditions and build along the mountain. There are four unique terraces in Yuanyang: the first is the large areas and various shapes of terraced fields stretching in **succession**[①]; the second is the steep terrains, which can be seen from the gentle slope of 15 degrees to the cliff of 75 degrees; the third is the number of stages, where more than 3,000 steps can be made on one slope; and the fourth is the high **altitude**[②], the terraces extending from the river valley to the mountains with an altitude of more than 2,000 meters. Hani Terraces are the brilliant masterpieces left behind by the Hani people from generation to generation.

哈尼梯田壮丽而独特。哈尼族开垦梯田,因地制宜,随山而建。元阳梯田有四绝:一是面积大,形状各异的梯田连绵成片;二是地势陡,从15度的缓坡到75度的峭壁上都能看见梯田;三是级数多,最多时能在一面坡上开出3000多级阶梯;四是海拔高,梯田由河谷一直延伸到海拔2000多米的山上。哈尼梯田是哈尼族人世世代代留下的辉煌杰作。

All the terraces in Yuanyang County are built on the hillsides, where the slope of the terraces **ranges**[③] from 15 to 75 degrees and the highest level of terraces reaches 3,000 steps. Hani Terraces mainly has three scenic spots, covering an area of tens of thousands of mu. These terraces are **spectacular**④ and breathtaking amid the forest and sea of clouds.

元阳县境内所有的梯田都建立在山坡上,梯田坡度在15到75度之间,梯田最高级数达3000级。哈尼梯田主要有三大景区,面积多达几万亩。这些梯田在森林和云海中蔚为壮观、令人惊叹。

Jingkou Folk Culture Village is a well-preserved natural village of the Hani people in Yuanyang County. It is built on the mountainside of terraced fields. These houses are built according to the mountains, looking like a sea of mushrooms. Here you can also enjoy the unique Hani **ethnic**⑤ song and dance performances.

箐口民俗村是元阳县境内保存完好的一个哈尼族自然村寨,它建在梯田的半山腰上,这些房子依山而建错落有致,放眼望去犹如一朵朵蘑菇浑然天成。在这里还可以欣赏到独具民族风情的哈尼族歌舞表演。

 佳句点睛　Punchlines

1. Hani Terraces have been a natural ecosystem full of **vitality**⑥ since ancient times.

哈尼梯田自古以来都是一个充满生命活力的自然生态系统。

2. Hani Terraces are the true art of the earth, a **veritable**⑦ sculp-

ture of the earth.

哈尼梯田是真正的大地艺术,是名副其实的大地雕塑。

3. Duoyishu Terraces are the best place to watch the sunrise. Duoyishu faces mountains on three sides and falls into a valley on one side, surrounded by clouds all year round.

多依树梯田是日出的最佳观赏地。多依树三面临山,一面坠入山谷,常年云雾缭绕。

情景对话 Situational Dialogue

A: Do you think Red River Hani Terraces are a vanity project?

B: No, it isn't. This is a farming civilization created by the Hani people using unique geographical and climatic conditions. It has been more than 1,300 years ago.

A: I thought it was a mere form.

B: It can be said that Hani Terraces are a model of harmony between man and nature.

A: Can you dwell on it?

B: Yes, I can. Hani Terraces are paddy fields, built accordng to the conditions of the mountain, the slope of the terraces ranges from 15 to 75 degrees, there are more than 3,000 steps from the foot of the mountain to the top of the mountain and there are often thousands of acres of terraced fields on a hillside. There's a saying that is very

graphic⑤, "The mountain gully is like a jade belt while the layers of terraced fields are like heavenly ladders".

A: That's great!

B: In fact, the Hani people did not **deliberately**⑥ pursue the artistic beauty of terraces when they built them. The role of terraces is to maintain water and soil, increase the area of cultivated land in mountainous areas, and achieve a relative balance between resource protection and utilization.

A: However, the Hani people have achieved unity of nature and human.

B: This is also the symbol of Hani's national spirit.

A: 你说红河哈尼梯田是不是面子工程啊？

B: 不，绝不是面子工程，这可是哈尼族人利用独特的地理气候条件创造的农耕文明，到现在已经1300多年了。

A: 我还以为是花架子呢。

B: 可以说，哈尼梯田是人与自然和谐的典范。

A: 你能说得具体一点吗？

B: 可以，哈尼梯田都是水田，是因地制宜随山而建的，梯田坡度在15至75度之间，从山脚到山顶层层叠叠多达3000余级，一个山坡上常常有成千上万亩梯田，有句话说得非常形象，就是"山间水沟如玉带，层层梯田似天梯"。

A: 说得太好了！

B: 其实，哈尼族修建梯田时并没有刻意追求梯田的艺术美感，梯田的作用就是为了保持水土,增加山区耕地的面积,在资源的保护和利用之间取得相对平衡。

A: 但是,哈尼族人做到了天人合一。

B: 这也正是哈尼民族精神的象征。

生词注解　Notes

① succession /sək'seʃn/　*n.* 连续;一连串

② altitude /'æltɪtjuːd/　*n.* 海拔;高度

③ range /reɪndʒ/　*v.* (在……内)变动

④ spectacular /spek'tækjələ(r)/　*adj.* 壮观的;引人入胜的

⑤ ethnic /'eθnɪk/　*adj.* 种族的;人种的

⑥ vitality /vaɪ'tæləti/　*n.* 活力;生命力

⑦ veritable /'verɪtəbl/　*adj.* 真正的;名副其实的

⑧ graphic /'græfɪk/　*adj.* 形象的;绘画似的

⑨ deliberately /dɪ'lɪbərətli/　*adv.* 故意地;谨慎地

可可西里自然保护区

Hoh Xil Nature Reserve

导入语 Lead-in

可可西里自然保护区位于青海省玉树藏族自治州西部,是中国建成的面积大、海拔高、野生动物资源丰富的自然保护区之一,是藏羚羊、野牦牛、藏野驴、藏原羚等珍稀野生动植物的栖息地。2017年,可可西里自然保护区被列入《世界自然遗产名录》。2017年8月29日,可可西里保护区内的索南达杰保护站正式开通卫星通信固定站,标志着可可西里已经成为中国四大无人区(罗布泊、阿尔金、可可西里和西藏羌塘)中第一个接入互联网的地区。

文化剪影 Cultural Outline

Hoh Xil Nature Reserve is located in Yushu Tibetan Autonomous Prefecture, Qinghai Province. It is a high mountain platform stretching across Qinghai, Xinjiang and Tibet. The nature reserve is **adjacent**[①] to Tibet in the west, Golmud Tanggula Township in the south, Xinjiang Uygur Autonomous Region in the north and Qinghai-Tibet Highway in the east, with a total area of 45,000 square kilometers.

可可西里自然保护区位于青海省玉树藏族自治州境内,是横跨青海、新疆、西藏之间的一块高山台地。自然保护区西与西藏相接,南与格尔木唐古拉乡毗邻,北与新疆维吾尔自治区相连,东到青藏公路,总面积4.5万平方千米。

Hoh Xil is divided into three water systems: the North Source outflow system of the Yangtze River composed of the Chumar River system in the east, which is mainly supplied by rainwater and groundwater, with a small amount of water, and chiefly by seasonal rivers; the east Qiangtang inner water system centered on lakes in the west and north, is located in the northeast of the inner flow lake area of the Qiangtang Plateau; and the middle part of the north is the inner water system of the Qaidam Basin, mainly by the Hongshui River, which flows into Qaidam Basin through the Kunlun Mountains.

可可西里分为三个水系:东部是楚玛尔河水系组成的长江北源

外流水系，主要以雨水、地下水补给，水量较小，以季节性河流为主；西部和北部是以湖泊为中心的东羌塘内流水系，处于羌塘高原内流湖区的东北部；北部中段是柴达木盆地内流水系，以红水河为主，穿越昆仑山流入柴达木盆地。

The soil types of the Hoh Xil Nature Reserve mainly include three zonal soils such as alpine meadow soil, alpine grassland soil and alpine cold desert soil. The next is marsh soil as well as scattered meadow soil, cracked soil, saline soil, **alkaline**② soil and **aeolian**③ sand and so on. The river basins in the protected area almost cover the entire protected area; there are many lakes, 107 lakes with an area of more than one square kilometer, 6 with an area of more than 200 square kilometers, and more than 7,000 with an area of less than one square kilometers, so it is known as "The Land of a Thousand Lakes".

可可西里自然保护区土壤的类型主要有高山草甸土、高山草原土和高山寒漠土三个地带性土壤。其次是沼泽土，零星分布的有草甸土、龟裂土、盐土、碱土和风沙土等。保护区内河水流域几乎遍及整个保护区；湖泊众多，面积大于1平方千米的湖泊有107个，面积在200平方公里以上的有6个，1平方千米以下的有7000多个，因此被称为"千湖之地"。

佳句点睛 Punchlines

1. The natural conditions in Hoh Xil are so harsh that people can't

live for a long time, but it's a paradise for wild animals.

可可西里自然条件恶劣，人类无法长期居住，但却是野生动物的天堂。

2. Hoh Xil lies in the northwest of the Tibetan Plateau, like a pearl **inlaid**① between the Tanggula Mountains and the Kunlun Mountains.

可可西里位于青藏高原西北部，像一颗明珠镶嵌在唐古拉山和昆仑山之间。

3. Hoh Xil Nature Reserve is one of the world's well-preserved areas of pristine ecology as well as the last natural place left in its primitive state.

可可西里自然保护区既是目前世界上原始生态环境保存较为完美的地区之一，也是最后一块保留着原始状态的自然地带。

 情景对话　**Situational Dialogue**

A: Is there a barrier around Hoh Xil Nature Reserve?

B: The terrain there is high and steep, so there are no barriers around it. It is one of the well-preserved areas of the original ecological environment in the world, and it is also the last natural area with its original state.

A: What about the natural conditions there?

B: The natural conditions there are harsh and humans can't live for a long time, but it is a paradise for wild animals.

A: What wild animals are there?

B: For example, wild **yaks**⑤, Tibetan antelopes, wild donkeys, white-lipped deer, and brown bears. These are all unique wild animals on the Qinghai-Tibet Plateau.

A: I've heard that Hoh Xil is currently one of the regions with rich animal resources in China, with over 230 wild animals.

B: Exactly. Among them, the Tibetan antelope is called the pride of Hoh Xil. It is a peculiar species in China, and also an **endangered**⑥ animal.

A: Are Tibetan antelopes particularly **vulnerable**⑦?

B: No, Tibetan antelopes are a kind of **dominant**⑧ animals, who often emerge in groups on the horizon after the first snowfall, graceful and elf-like.

A: 可可西里自然保护区周围有没有屏障？

B: 那里地势高峻，周围没有任何屏障，是世界上原始生态环境保存较为完美的地区之一，也是最后一块保留着原始状态的自然地带。

A: 那里自然条件怎么样？

B: 自然条件恶劣，人类无法长期居住，但却是野生动物的天堂。

A: 都有哪些野生动物？

B: 比如野牦牛、藏羚羊、野驴、白唇鹿、棕熊，这些都是青藏高原上特有的野生动物。

A：我听说可可西里目前是中国动物资源较为丰富的地区之一，拥有的野生动物多达230多种。

B：没错。其中，藏羚羊被称为可可西里的骄傲，它是我国特有的物种，也是濒危动物。

A：藏羚羊是不是特别脆弱？

B：不，藏羚羊是一种优势动物，它们常常成群结队地出现在雪后初霁的地平线上，姿态优美，像精灵一般。

生词注解　Notes

① adjacent /əˈdʒeɪsnt/　*adj.* 邻近的；毗连的

② alkaline /ˈælkəlaɪn/　*adj.* 碱性的；含碱的

③ aeolian /iːˈəʊlɪən/　*adj.* 风成的；风积的

④ inlay /ˌɪnˈleɪ/　*vt.* 把……嵌入；把……镶入

⑤ yak /jæk/　*n.* 牦牛

⑥ endangered /ɪnˈdeɪndʒəd/　*adj.* 濒临灭绝的

⑦ vulnerable /ˈvʌlnərəbl/　*adj.* 脆弱的；不堪一击的

⑧ dominant /ˈdɒmɪnənt/　*adj.* 占优势的；支配的

珠穆朗玛峰

Mount Qomolangma

导入语　Lead-in

珠穆朗玛峰是喜马拉雅山脉的主峰，也是世界第一高峰。"珠穆朗玛"在藏语里是"圣母"的意思。珠穆朗玛峰峰顶位于中国与尼泊尔的边界，南坡位于尼泊尔萨加玛塔专区，北坡位于中国西藏自治区定日县。中华人民共和国第四版人民币十元纸币的背面便是珠穆朗玛峰。2020年12月8日，中国与尼泊尔共同宣布珠穆朗玛峰最新高度为8848.86米。

文化剪影　Cultural Outline

Mount Qomolangma is a giant **pyramid**①, with steep terrain and complex environment. Between the ridges and cliffs are 548 continental glaciers with an average thickness of 7,260 meters. On the glacier there are various kinds of **serac**② bands and dangerous ice **avalanche**③ zones.

珠穆朗玛峰山体呈巨型金字塔状,地形险峻,环境复杂。山脊和峭壁之间分布着548条大陆型冰川,平均厚度7260米。冰川上有千姿百态的冰塔林和险象环生的冰崩区。

Mount Qomolangma has a unique geographical environment. The lowest temperature on the summit is minus 30 degrees **Celsius**④ all the year round. Snow does not melt all year round, glaciers, ice slopes, ice tower scattering everywhere. The air at the summit is thin, often blowing seven or eight strong wind while force twelve strong wind is not uncommon. The wind blows the **drifts**⑤ dancing in the sky.

珠穆朗玛峰地理环境独特,峰顶的最低气温常年在零下三十摄氏度。积雪常年不融化,冰川、冰坡、冰塔林随处可见。峰顶空气稀薄,经常刮七八级大风,十二级大风也不少见。风吹积雪,漫天飞舞。

Mount Qomolangma is **majestic**⑥ and magnificent, with numerous ranges upon ranges of peaks and mountains, more than 40 peaks over 7,000 meters above sea level forming a spectacular scene of **myriads**[7] of peaks coming towards and surging at the peak head.

珠穆朗玛峰巍峨宏大,气势磅礴,群峰林立,山峦叠障,海拔7000米以上的高峰有40多座,形成了群峰来朝、峰头汹涌的壮观场面。

佳句点睛 Punchlines

1. The towering image of Mount Qomolangma has had a major impact on a worldwide scale.

珠穆朗玛峰高大巍峨的形象一直在世界范围内产生重大的影响。

2. The five peaks of the Himalayas, headed by Mount Qomolangma, are the five fairies, known as the "Five Fairies of **Longevity**[8]".

喜马拉雅山以珠穆朗玛峰为首的五座山峰是仙女五姐妹,被誉为"长寿五仙女"。

3. On the north side of Mount Qomolangma are two gigantic glaciers, like two silvery dragons running down into the valley.

珠穆朗玛峰北面有两条巨大的冰川,就像两条银龙直入山谷。

情景对话 Situational Dialogue

A: Have you ever seen the flag clouds on Mount Qomolangma? On clear days, the milky clouds like flags often floating on the summit of Mount Qomolangma.

B: What's the use of flag clouds?

A: The flag clouds can be used as a weather **vane**① and can also forecast the weather according to its direction.

B: What causes the flag clouds on Qomolangma?

A: Because of the high altitude of Mount Qomolangma, strong solar radiation and uneven heating, the surface temperature of the fast absorbing area is higher than the free atmosphere at the same height and the formation of air flow up the hillside. In addition, on the surface of snow and ice, as the cold air sinks and the hot air rises, the local circulations occur in two different directions, creating **convective**② cumulus clouds near the summit, so that the banner-like clouds are often visibly suspended at the summit during the day.

B: It's amazing.

A: There's something even more amazing.

B: Oh, what is it?

A: It's the ice table. It's an icicle with a huge stone on top of it, like a table with a wonderful structure.

B: How did it come about?

风景名胜

A: Because the ice covered by the rocks is protected from melting, it is held high and the unprotected ice around it is lowered by rapid melting, thus forming an ice table.

B: That's really worthy of Mount Qomolangma!

A: 你见过珠穆朗玛峰的旗云吗？就是天气晴朗时，珠峰顶经常飘浮着像旗帜一样的乳白色烟云。

B: 旗云有什么作用？

A: 旗云既可以作为风向标，也可以根据方向变化预报天气。

B: 珠穆朗玛峰为什么会产生旗云呢？

A: 因为它海拔高，太阳辐射强，各地受热不均，在吸热快的地区，表层气温高于同一高度自由大气的温度，所以就形成了沿山坡向上的气流。此外，在冰雪面上，冷空气下沉，热空气上升，就会产生两个方向不同的局部环流，使峰顶附近形成对流性积云，因此白天常常能观测到像旗帜一样的云挂在峰顶。

B: 太神奇了。

A: 还有更神奇的呢。

B: 噢，是什么？

A: 冰桌，就是一根冰柱顶着一块大石头，酷似结构奇妙的桌子。

B: 这又是怎么形成的呢？

A: 被石块遮挡的冰块不易消融，所以高高擎起，周围未受遮挡的冰面因消融很快而变低，于是就这样形成了冰桌。

B: 真不愧是珠穆朗玛峰！

生词注解　Notes

① pyramid /ˈpɪrəmɪd/　*n.* 金字塔；角锥体

② serac /səˈræk/　*n.* 冰塔

③ avalanche /ˈævəlɑːnʃ/　*n.* 雪崩

④ Celsius /ˈselsɪəs/　*n.* 摄氏度

⑤ drift /drɪft/　*n.*（吹积成的）雪堆

⑥ majestic /məˈdʒestɪk/　*adj.* 庄严的；宏伟的

⑦ myriad /ˈmɪrɪəd/　*n.* 无数；极大数量

⑧ longevity /lɒnˈdʒevətɪ/　*n.* 长寿；长命

⑨ vane /veɪn/　*n.* 风向标；风信旗

⑩ convective /kəˈvektɪv/　*adj.* 对流的；传递性的

风景名胜

新疆天山

The Tianshan Mountains in Xinjiang

 导入语 Lead-in

新疆地域宽广,资源丰富,拥有独一无二的自然和文化遗产资源。世界七大山系的天山是全球温带干旱区最大的山系,呈东西走向,绵延中国境内1700千米,面积57万多平方千米,约占新疆全区面积的三分之一,具有得天独厚的自然奇观,典型的山地垂直自然带谱、南北坡景观差异和植物多样性展示了帕米尔-天山山地生物生态的演进过程,这里也是中亚山地众多珍稀濒危物种和特有物种最重要的栖息地。2013年,新疆天山被列入《世界自然遗产名录》,这对更好地保护和传承珍贵的自然和人文资源具有非常重要的现实意义和社会价值。

自 然 景 观 第一部分

 文化剪影　Cultural Outline

The Tianshan Mountains in Xinjiang refers to the eastern part of the Tianshan Mountains and is also the main part of the Tianshan Mountains, whose areas include the Kashgar Region of Southern Xinjiang, the Kizilsu Kirgiz Autonomous **Prefecture**①, the Aksu Region, the Bayingoreng Mongolia Autonomous Prefecture, Turpan City, Hami City as well as the northern Xinjiang's Ili Kazakh Autonomous Prefecture, Boltala Mongolia Autonomous Prefecture, Shihezi City, Changji Hui Autonomous Prefecture and Urumqi City.

新疆天山是指天山山脉东段,也是天山山脉的主体部分,天山山区包括南疆的喀什地区、克孜勒苏柯尔克孜自治州、阿克苏地区、巴音郭楞蒙古自治州、吐鲁番市、哈密市,以及北疆的伊犁哈萨克自治州、博尔塔拉蒙古自治州、石河子市、昌吉回族自治州和乌鲁木齐市。

The Tianshan Mountains in Xinjiang span the entire territory of Xinjiang. It is the natural geographical boundary between the Junggar Basin and the Tarim Basin and a unique symbol of Xinjiang's geography.

新疆天山横跨新疆全境,它是准噶尔盆地和塔里木盆地的天然地理分界,也是新疆地理的独特标志。

The Tianshan Mountains in Xinjiang **prominently**② represent the biological evolution process of this region, which has been gradually

087

replaced by warm and wet flora by modern **xerophytic**③ Mediterranean **flora**④.

新疆天山集中体现了该区域由暖湿植物区系逐步被现代旱生的地中海植物区系替代的生物进化过程。

佳句点睛　Punchlines

1. Looking at Tianshan from afar, the snow-covered peaks that stick into the sky all year round are sparkling like the bead, silvery crowns of Uyghur girls.

远望天山,终年积雪、直插云霄的群峰,犹如维吾尔族少女的珠冠,银光闪闪。

2. Among the colorful water and stones, the shimmering **scales**⑤ of the fishes reflect the clear stream of snow and water, adding infinite vitality to the silent Tianshan.

在五彩斑斓的水石间,鱼群的闪闪鳞光映着雪水清流,给寂静的天山增添了无限生机。

3. Below the snow line of the peaks is the winding **verdant**⑥ forest, the dense Himalayan cedar are exactly like a giant umbrella that supports the sky.

群峰的雪线以下是蜿蜒翠绿的原始森林,浓密的塔松酷似撑天的巨伞。

情景对话 Situational Dialogue

A: Is Tianchi of the Tianshan Mountains in Xinjiang a fairyland of Yaochi?

B: It's a **mythological** and legend of course, but it's really a rare tourist attraction. It's a world-famous mountain lake.

A: Then you say that the mythological legends are not groundless?

B: Certainly not. It just gives the beautiful natural scenery of Tianchi a layer of mystery. In summer, it is an ideal summer **resort** with beautiful mountains and rivers, fresh and pleasant, where people can climb mountains, go through dense forests, or go boating on lakes to enjoy the scenery of lakes and mountains. In winter, there are snow-capped, silver-wrapped, and the lakes are as solid as jade. It is the rare **alpine** skating **rinks** in China.

A: Oh, really? What other wonders are there?

B: There're a lot more. For example, "Heavenly Mirror Floating in the Sky" "Key Stand" "Reflection in the Great Bay" "Sail in the Yaochi" and "Flying Waterfall in the Hanging Spring", and so on.

A: It sounds like a poetic place!

B: Xinjiang is a good place, not a false name.

A: 新疆天山的天池是不是瑶池仙境?

B: 这当然是神话传说,但那里的确是不可多得的游览胜地,是

风景名胜

世界著名的高山湖泊。

A: 神话传说是空穴来风吗?

B: 当然不是,只是给优美的天池自然景色蒙上了一层神秘的面纱。到了夏季,那里山清水秀,清爽宜人,是理想的避暑胜地。人们可以登高山、穿密林,也可以泛舟湖上、饱览湖光山色。到了冬天,那里白雪皑皑,银装素裹,湖上坚冰如玉,是全国少有的高山滑冰场。

A: 噢,是吗? 那里还有哪些奇观?

B: 多了去了。比如"天镜浮空""定海神针""大湾倒影""瑶池风帆""悬泉飞瀑"等等。

A: 听上去真是一个诗情画意的地方!

B: 新疆是个好地方,绝非浪得虚名。

生词注解 Notes

① prefecture /ˈpriːfektʃə(r)/ n. 管区;辖区

② prominently /ˈprɒmɪnəntlɪ/ adv. 显著地;突出地

③ xerophytic /ˌzɪərəʊˈfɪtɪk/ adj. 旱生性的;耐旱性的

④ flora /ˈflɔːrə/ n. 植物区系;植物群

⑤ scale /skeɪl/ n. 鳞;天平

⑥ verdant /ˈvɜːdnt/ adj. 青翠的;翠绿的

⑦ mythological /ˌmɪθəˈlɒdʒɪkl/ adj. 神话的;神话学的

⑧ resort /rɪˈzɔːt/ n. 度假胜地;常去之地

⑨ alpine /ˈælpaɪn/ adj. 高山的;(尤指瑞士境内的)高山的

⑩ rink /rɪŋk/ n. 溜冰场;室内溜冰场

自然景观 第一部分

长江三峡

The Three Gorges of the Yangtze River

 导入语　Lead-in

　　长江三峡西起重庆市奉节县白帝城，东至湖北省宜昌市南津关，横穿重庆奉节、巫山和湖北巴东、秭归、宜昌，全长193千米，由瞿塘峡、巫峡、西陵峡组成，被誉为"天然画廊"和"人间仙境"。瞿塘峡雄伟险峻，巫峡秀美幽深，西陵峡礁石林立、江流湍急，小三峡郁郁葱葱、清澈见底。两岸有众多的名胜古迹和优美动人的传说，构成一幅"高峡出平湖"的恢弘美景。长江三峡深谷曾是三国古战场，无数英雄豪杰曾在此雄姿英发，叱咤风云。长江三峡是世界大峡谷之一，也是中国十大风景名胜之一。

风景名胜

文化剪影 Cultural Outline

The Three Gorges of the Yangtze River is located on the main-**stream**① of the Yangtze River in the regions of Chongqing, Enshi and Yichang, starting from White Emperor Town in Fengjie County, Chongqing City, and reaching Nanjin Pass in Yichang City, Hubei Province. It is the most beautiful landscape gallery on the Yangtze River, consists of Qutang Gorge, Wuxia Gorge and Xiling Gorge.

长江三峡位于重庆、恩施、宜昌地区境内的长江干流上，西起重庆市奉节县的白帝城，东至湖北省宜昌市的南津关，由瞿塘峡、巫峡和西陵峡组成，是长江上最奇丽壮美的山水画廊。

Relying on the world's largest water **conservancy**② project—the Three Gorges Project, the Three Gorges Dam Tourist Area provides tourists with multi-functional services integrating tourism, science and education, leisure and entertainment, combining modern projects, natural scenery and human culture, and becoming a **desirable**③ tourist attraction.

三峡大坝旅游区以世界上最大的水利枢纽工程——三峡工程为依托，为游客提供了集游览、科教、休闲、娱乐于一体的多功能服务，将现代工程、自然风光和人文景观有机结合在一起，成为令人向往的旅游胜地。

Wuxia Gorge, also known as "Daxia (Great Gorge)", is famous for its depth and beauty, starting from the Daning River **estuary**① in the east of Wushan County in the west, and to the Guandu estuary in Badong County in the east. The continuous peaks, strange rocks, and cliffs of the whole gorge area are the most worthwhile section of the Three Gorges, like a gallery filled with thousands of turns and extremely beautiful scenery.

巫峡又名"大峡",以幽深秀美著称,西起巫山县城东面的大宁河口,东至巴东县官渡口。整个峡区奇峰、怪石、峭壁绵延不断,是三峡中最值得一看的一段,就像一条千回百转、美不胜收的画廊。

佳句点睛 Punchlines

1. The Goddess Peak stands among the **towering**⑤ mountains on the north bank of the Yangtze River, like a young girl, slim and graceful.

神女峰耸立在长江北岸巍峨的群山中,犹如一位少女亭亭玉立。

2. When the peak is **shrouded**⑥ in mist, the human-shaped stone pillars seem to be covered with **gauze**⑦, full of affection, charming, moving and graceful.

峰顶云雾缭绕时,人形石柱仿佛披上了薄纱,含情脉脉,妩媚动人,婀娜多姿。

3. On the north bank of the Yangtze River is a **stack**⑧ of layered

rocks that look like a pile of thick books, and a thick, pointy stone pillar pointing toward the middle of the river, much like a sword.

长江北岸有一叠层次分明的岩石，看上去像一堆厚书，还有一根上粗下尖的石柱指向江中，酷似一把宝剑。

情景对话　Situational Dialogue

A: It's well-known that the Yangtze River is the largest river in China. Do you know where it **originated**⑨?

B: Of course I do. It originated from the southwestern side of the Gradanton Peak in the Tanggula Mountains in Qinghai Province.

A: Did the Yellow River also originate from there?

B: No, it originated from the Bayan Har Mountains on the Qinghai-Tibet Plateau.

A: Both rivers are mother rivers of the Chinese nation, right?

B: Yes. The two rivers, one south and one north, gave birth to the ancient Chinese civilization.

A: There're Three Gorges in the Yangtze River. Do you know which Three Gorges are?

B: Qutang Gorge, Wuxia Gorge and Xiling Gorge.

A: The most **commendable**⑩ is the Yangtze River Three Gorges Water Conservancy Project.

B: Yeah, it's a great livehood project since the establishment of the People's Republic of China.

自然景观

A: 众所周知,长江是我国的第一大河。你知道它发源于哪里吗?

B: 当然知道,它发源于青海省唐古拉山脉各拉丹冬峰西南侧。

A: 黄河是不是也发源于那里?

B: 不是,黄河发源于青海省青藏高原巴颜喀拉山脉。

A: 两条河流都是中华民族的母亲河,这没错吧?

B: 是的。两条河流一南一北,共同孕育了古老的华夏文明。

A: 长江有三峡,你知道是哪三峡吗?

B: 瞿塘峡、巫峡和西陵峡。

A: 还有最值得称道的是长江三峡水利枢纽工程。

B: 是啊,这可是新中国一项伟大的民生工程。

生词注解 Notes

① mainstream /ˈmeɪnstriːm/　　n. 主流

② conservancy /kənˈsɜːvənsɪ/　　n. 保护;保存

③ desirable /dɪˈzaɪərəbl/　　adj. 可取的;令人向往的

④ estuary /ˈestʃuərɪ/　　n. 河口;江口

⑤ towering /ˈtaʊərɪŋ/　　adj. 高耸的;峥嵘的

⑥ shroud /ʃraʊd/　　vt. 笼罩;覆盖

⑦ gauze /gɔːz/　　n. 薄纱;薄雾

⑧ stack /stæk/　　n. (整齐的)一堆;(干草或谷物的)堆

⑨ originate /əˈrɪdʒɪneɪt/　　vi. 发源;起源

⑩ commendable /kəˈmendəbl/　　adj. 值得称道的;值得赞扬的

西湖

The West Lake

导入语 Lead-in

西湖最早被称为"武林水",古称"钱塘湖",又名"西子湖",位于浙江省杭州市区西部,以秀丽的湖光山色和众多的名胜古迹而闻名遐迩。西湖是中国主要的观赏性淡水湖泊,也是中国首批国家重点风景名胜区,更是中国著名的旅游胜地,拥有"一山、二塔、三岛、三堤、五湖"的山水与人文交融的格调,被誉为"人间天堂"。西湖是中国十大风景名胜之一,也是目前中国唯一被列入《世界遗产名录》的湖泊类文化遗产。

文化剪影　Cultural Outline

The West Lake covers an area of 60 square kilometers and the surface of the lake is 5.68 square kilometers. The scenic area is surrounded by the mountains on three sides. The ancient stone bridges **span**[1] the lake. Whether it is in spring, summer, autumn and winter or windy, frosty, snowy and rainy, it has its own unique charm.

西湖面积60平方千米，湖面5.68平方千米。风景区以秀丽雅致的西湖为中心，三面环山，古石桥横跨湖上，无论春夏秋冬还是风霜雪雨，景色都别有一番风味。

The beauty of the West Lake lies in its **lingering**[2] charm. Among the beautiful scenic spots, the most famous is the ten sceneries of the West Lake. Unique is each scenic spot, which shows the **essence**[3] of the West Lake scenery and **constitutes**[4] the core of the West Lake tourism.

西湖之美在于韵味。在美景中，最著名的是西湖十景。每个景点都独一无二，展现了西湖风景的精华，构成了西湖旅游的核心。

The West Lake is a natural picture. In March, the grass grows and the **orioles**[5] fly, the peach and willow trees are lined on the either side of the bank, the waves **ripple**[6], the cruises are dotted, the mountains are empty and misty, and the natural indigo merges with **verdancy**[7].

风景名胜

It's **intoxicating**®, just as we walk into a fairyland on earth.

西湖是一幅天然图画,阳春三月,草长莺飞,桃柳夹岸,水波潋滟,游船点点,山色空蒙,青黛含翠,令人心醉神迷,犹如走进了人间仙境。

 ## 佳句点睛　Punchlines

1. The West Lake is like a shining pearl inlaid at the mouth of the beautiful and fertile Hangzhou Bay.

西湖就像一颗璀璨的明珠,镶嵌在美丽富饶的杭州湾口。

2. As it is beautiful all the year round, Su Dongpo, a well-known poet of the Song Dynasty, praised the West Lake with his line of "being always charming with either light or heavy makeup".

西湖一年四季都美不胜收,宋代著名诗人苏东坡用"淡妆浓抹总相宜"的诗句来赞誉西湖。

3. The West Lake has not only the beautiful landscape, but also the rich cultural relics and historical sites and beautiful fairy tales.

西湖既有秀丽的山水,又有丰富的文物古迹和优美动人的神话传说。

情景对话 Situational Dialogue

A: It's so beautiful here.

B: Yes, Hangzhou has always been known as "The Paradise on Earth". Ancient Chinese people praised the area around the West Lake as a **miraculous** and beautiful land. In modern times, the West Lake is regarded as the pride of Hangzhou, and a perfect spot to escape the hustle and **bustle** of the city.

A: Let's visit the West Lake first, shall we?

B: OK.

A: Where are we now?

B: Here is Viewing Fish at the Flower Pond.

A: Could we go boating on the West Lake?

B: Of course. We'll see the Three Pools Mirroring the Moon soon. There are three small stone towers rising from the lake. On the night of the Mid-autumn Festival, people put candles inside. The candle-light reflects the reflection on the water, much like the shadow of the moon.

A: Really wonderful!

B: And mysterious.

A: 这里真是太美了。

B: 是的，杭州一向被誉为"人间天堂"。中国古代人民将西湖周边誉为神奇美丽的土地。在现代，西湖被视为杭州的骄傲，是人们躲

风景名胜

避城市喧嚣的绝佳去处。

A: 我们先去游览西湖,好不好?

B: 好啊。

A: 我们眼下在哪里?

B: 这里是花港观鱼。

A: 我们可以在西湖上划船吗?

B: 当然可以。我们马上就可以看到三潭印月了。湖中有三个高出水面的小石塔。中秋之夜,人们在石塔内放上蜡烛,烛光反射到水面上,很像月亮的倒影。

A: 真奇妙!

B: 也很神秘。

生词注解 Notes

① span /spæn/ *vt.* 跨越;持续

② lingering /ˈlɪŋgərɪŋ/ *adj.* 继续存留的;久久不散的

③ essence /ˈesns/ *n.* 精华;本质

④ constitute /ˈkɒnstɪtjuːt/ *vt.* 构成;组成

⑤ oriole /ˈɔːrɪəʊl/ *n.* 黄鹂

⑥ ripple /ˈrɪpl/ *vi.* 起涟漪

⑦ verdancy /ˈvɜːdnsɪ/ *n.* 青翠;翠绿

⑧ intoxicating /ɪnˈtɒksɪkeɪtɪŋ/ *adj.* 醉人的;令人陶醉的

⑨ miraculous /mɪˈrækjələs/ *adj.* 奇迹般的;超自然的

⑩ hustle and bustle   熙熙攘攘

庐山

Mount Lu

导入语 Lead-in

庐山,又名"匡山""匡庐",是一座风景秀丽、底蕴深厚、历史悠久的文化名山,以雄、奇、险、秀而闻名遐迩。在此,陶渊明创作了《桃花源记》,李白写下了《望庐山瀑布》,周敦颐吟出了《爱莲说》,

苏轼慨叹"不识庐山真面目,只缘身在此山中"。毛泽东赋诗"天生一个仙人洞,无限风光在险峰"。白居易以"匡庐奇秀甲天下"道出了庐山的秀美和品位。庐山是世界地质公园、全国重点文物保护单位、国家重点风景名胜区、国家5A级旅游景区、世界著名避暑胜地和首批全国文明风景旅游区示范点。1996年,庐山被联合国教科文组织列入《世界文化遗产名录》。

风 景 名 胜

文化剪影 Cultural Outline

Mount Lu is 36 kilometers away from Jiujiang City, Jiangxi Province, bordering the Yangtze River in the north and the Poyang Lake in the east, covering an area of 350 square kilometers. As one of the cradles of Chinese civilization, it has been known as "majesty, mystery, **precipitousness**① and beauty" since ancient times.

庐山距江西省九江市36千米,北临长江,东濒鄱阳湖,方圆350平方千米,是中华文明的发祥地之一,自古便以"雄奇险秀"而闻名。

The perfect combination of natural scenery and historic buildings in Mount Lu has created a unique cultural landscape that embodies the extraordinary **aesthetic**② value of Chinese spiritual and cultural life, and has become a **microcosm**③ of Chinese national spirit and cultural life.

庐山自然风光和历史建筑的完美结合,创造了一种独特的文化景观,体现了中国精神文化生活非凡的审美价值,已经成为中国民族精神和文化生活的缩影。

The Buddhist and Taoist temples in Mount Lu, as well as the landmarks of Confucianism, are fully **integrated**④ into the natural beauty of the landscape and have inspired countless artists.

庐山的佛教和道教庙观,以及儒学的里程碑建筑,完全融合在美不胜收的自然景观当中,赋予了无数艺术家创作的灵感。

佳句点睛 Punchlines

1. Mount Lu sits on the south bank of the Yangtze River, its 90-odd peaks rising and falling like a row of **screens**⑤.

庐山雄踞长江南岸,绵延起伏的90多座山峰,就像一扇扇屏风。

2. Mount Lu is a wonderful reflection and historical **epitome**⑥ of Chinese landscape culture. The nature of Mount Lu is poetic and humanized.

庐山是中国山水文化的精彩折射和历史缩影。庐山的自然既是诗化的,也是人化的。

3. Mount Lu enjoys the **prestige**⑦ of "being the most wonderful and beautiful in the world", which is of high tourism value.

庐山享有"匡庐奇秀甲天下山"的盛誉,具有极高的旅游观赏价值。

情景对话 Situational Dialogue

A: I learned Su Shi's *Written on the Wall at West Forest Temple* in school. And I'm really curious about the scene in the poem.

B: I learned it, too. The scene **depicted**⑧ in the poem is really so

风景名胜

beautiful that I desire to see the waterfall of Mount Lu.

A: Mount Lu Waterfall Group is one of the beautiful waterfalls in China. Scholars and poets of all dynasties have written poems and **inscriptions**① in praise of its majesty and magnificence.

B: The most famous poem is Li Bai's *Gazing at the Waterfall in Mount Lu*, which has been a poetic masterpiece through the ages.

A: And the White Deer **Grotto**② Academy was one of the four great academies in ancient China, and Mount Lu is one of the cradles of Chinese civilization.

B: I know it. And there're many beautiful and moving legends.

A: Right.

A: 我在学校学习了苏轼的《题西林壁》。我对诗中的场景很好奇。

B: 我也学了这首诗,诗中描绘的景象实在是太美了,我真的想看庐山瀑布。

A: 庐山瀑布群是中国秀丽的瀑布之一。历代文人墨客在此赋诗题词,纷纷赞颂其壮观雄伟。

B: 最有名的当属李白的《望庐山瀑布》,早已成为千古绝唱。

A: 此外,白鹿洞书院是中国古代四大书院之一,而且江西庐山也是中华文明的发祥地之一。

B: 这我知道。那里还有好多美丽动人的传说呢。

A: 没错。

生词注解　Notes

① precipitousness /prɪˈsɪpɪtəsnəs/　n. 险峻

② aesthetic /iːsˈθetɪk/　adj. 美学的；审美的

③ microcosm /ˈmaɪkrəʊkɒzəm/　n. 微观世界；小宇宙

④ integrate /ˈɪntɪɡreɪt/　vi. 成为一体

⑤ screen /skriːn/　n. 屏风；屏幕

⑥ epitome /ɪˈpɪtəmaɪz/　n. 缩影；摘要

⑦ prestige /preˈstiːʒ/　n. 威望；声望

⑧ depict /dɪˈpɪkt/　vt. 描述；描绘

⑨ inscription /ɪnˈskrɪpʃn/　n. 题词；题字

⑩ grotto /ˈɡrɑːtəʊ/　n.（吸引人的）岩洞；洞穴

五台山

Mount Wutai

导入语 Lead-in

五台山是中国唯一的青庙与黄庙共存的佛教道场,位居中国四大佛教名山之首,被称为"金五台"。68年,山上开始修寺庙,历经整个唐代,最终成为中国古代建筑珍宝。在长达十五个世纪的发展中,五台山逐渐形成了规模宏大的佛教建筑群。这里是文殊菩萨的道场,具有悠久的佛教历史,与浙江普陀山、安徽九华山、四川峨眉山合称"中国佛教四大名山"。五台山与尼泊尔蓝毗尼花园、印度鹿野苑、菩提伽耶和拘尸那迦合称为"世界五大佛教圣地"。五台山也是中国十大名山之一,2009年被联合国教科文组织列入《世界文化遗产名录》。

自然景观 第一部分

 文化剪影 Cultural Outline

Mount Wutai is located in the northeast corner of Wutai County, Xinzhou City, Shanxi Province. Mount Wutai is not a mountain, but a series of peaks located on the "Roof of North China". The five peaks (Wanghai Peak, Jinxiu Peak, Cuiyan Peak, Guayue Peak and Yedou Peak) surround the whole area. There is no forest on the top of the mountain. It's as flat and broad as a platform built on earth, so it was named.

五台山位于山西省忻州市五台县东北隅，五台山并非一座山，而是坐落于"华北屋脊"之上的一系列山峰群。五座山峰（望海峰、锦绣峰、翠岩峰、挂月峰、叶斗峰）环抱整片区域，山顶没有林木，平坦开阔，就像垒土之台，故而得名。

Mount Wutai is the oldest preserved wooden building in China since the Tang Dynasty. With its unique natural and cultural heritage value, it is **showcasing**① its vastness and magnificence to the world.

五台山是中国自唐朝以来保存最古老的木制建筑胜地。五台山正以独特的自然与文化遗产价值，向世界展示其博大和瑰丽。

Mount Wutai is the most **typical**② Chinese royal Taoism center. Among the four famous Buddhist mountains in China, it is most closely related to the **centralized**③ capitals such as Xi'an, Luoyang, Kaifeng and Beijing.

五台山是最典型的中国皇家道场,在中国佛教四大名山中,五台山与历代帝都联系最为密切,如西安、洛阳、开封、北京等。

 佳句点睛　Punchlines

1. The pleasant weather and the natural scenery make Mount Wutai an ideal summer **resort**④.

宜人的气候和自然的风光,使五台山成为理想的避暑胜地。

2. Mount Wutai has become the residence of the Bodhisattva of **Manjusri**⑤ faith that still has a **profound**⑥ influence to this day.

五台山已经成为文殊菩萨的道场,至今仍有深远影响。

3. Mount Wutai has an outstanding position in the history of Chinese art, and is an ideal physical example of the **sinicization**⑦ of Buddhist art.

五台山在中国美术史上地位突出,是佛教艺术中国化的理想实物例证。

 情景对话　Situational Dialogue

A: We'll have a vacation next month. Why not have a tour?
B: Good idea. Where shall we go?

A: What about going to Shanxi?

B: Why do you wanna visit Shanxi?

A: Because I've heard it is so beautiful and has its own special feature.

B: Can you tell me something about it?

A: Okay. Wanghai Peak in the east is a good place to watch the sunrise and the sea of clouds. Jinxiu Peak in the south is a sea of flowers. Guayue Peak in the west is a good place to admire the moon, where the cool moonlight has a special charm. Yedou Peak in the north is the highest peak of Mount Wutai, known as "the Roof of North China". And Cuiyan Peak in the middle is magnificent with many **celestial**® wonders.

B: That's great!

A：我们下个月有假期。为什么不去旅游呢？

B：好主意，去哪里呢？

A：去山西怎么样？

B：你为什么想去山西呢？

A：我听说那里非常漂亮，颇具特色。

B：你能给我讲讲吗？

A：好的。东台望海峰是观赏日出云海的好地方。南台锦绣峰是花的海洋。西台挂月峰是赏月的绝佳之处，清凉的月光别有一番韵味。北台叶斗峰是五台山的最高峰，被称为"华北屋脊"。中台翠岩峰则是一座雄伟的山峰，那里有很多天造奇观。

风景名胜

B: 太棒了！

 生词注解 Notes

① showcase /ˈʃəʊkeɪs/　*vt.* 展现；表现

② typical /ˈtɪpɪkl/　*adj.* 典型的；特有的

③ centralized /ˈsentrəlaɪzd/　*adj.* 中央集权的；集中的

④ resort /rɪˈzɔːt/　*n.* 度假胜地

⑤ Manjusri /ˈmændʒuʃrɪ/　*n.* 文殊菩萨

⑥ profound /prəˈfaʊnd/　*adj.* 深厚的；意义深远的

⑦ sinicization /ˌsɪnəsaɪˈzeɪʃn/　*n.* 中国化

⑧ celestial /səˈlestɪəl/　*adj.* 天上的；天空的

第二部分 文化遗产

Part Ⅱ Cultural Landscape

长城

The Great Wall

导入语　Lead-in

长城始建于春秋战国时期，秦始皇统一中国后逐步扩建成了万里长城，汉朝和明朝也都进行了大规模修筑。墙身是城墙的主要部分，平均高度为7.8米，有些地段高达14米，长城上设置有大量烽火台，是古代的重要军事防御设施，也是冷兵器战争时代的国家军事性防御工程，堪称世界奇迹。在长城的所有景观中，北京八达岭长城建筑最坚固、保存最完好，也是长城的最佳观赏点。著名的长城关口有嘉峪关、山海关、居庸关、玉门关、娘子关、雁门关、平型关等。长城不仅是中华民族一脉相承、历史悠久的伟大象征，也是人类文明蓬勃发展的有力见证。

风景名胜

文化剪影　Cultural Outline

The Great Wall is located in the northern part of China, starting from Shanhai Pass in the east and Jiayu Pass in the west. It is an ancient military defense project with the longest construction time and the largest amount of work in the world. It is praised as "**spanning**① two thousand years and covering ten thousand li". The Great Wall is not only one of the Seven Wonders of the World, but also a symbol of the Chinese nation.

长城位于中国北方地区,东起山海关,西至嘉峪关,是世界上修建时间最长、工程量最大的一项古代军事防御工程,被誉为"上下两千年,纵横十万里"。长城既是"世界七大奇迹"之一,也是中华民族的象征。

The Great Wall is like a giant dragon, running from the west to the east, passing through the deserts, over the mountains, across the valleys, winding and rolling and **stretching**② for thousands of miles, which can be called a **miracle**③ of the world.

长城像一条巨龙,由西到东,穿沙漠、越高山、跨山谷、蜿蜒起伏、绵延万里,堪称世界奇迹。

The **architectural**① value of the Great Wall is comparable to its historical and **strategic**② importance, and bears witness to the enduring faith that the Chinese nation has stood firm despite the **vicissitudes**⑥ of history.

长城在建筑上的价值足以与其在历史和战略上的重要性相媲美，也见证了中华民族历经沧桑、始终屹立不倒的坚定信念。

佳句点睛　Punchlines

1. Lots of legends and stories about the Great Wall took place along its construction.

许多关于长城的传说和故事都是伴随着长城的修建而产生的。

2. From a distance, the Badaling Great Wall looks like a long dragon **winding**⑦ its way through the mountains.

从远处看，八达岭长城仿佛一条蜿蜒穿梭在崇山峻岭当中的长龙。

3. The Great Wall is a precious cultural **heritage**⑧ of mankind, shining everywhere with the light of Chinese civilization and wisdom.

长城是人类珍贵的文化遗产，处处都闪耀着中华民族文明和智慧的光芒。

情景对话　Situational Dialogue

A: I've heard you're making plans about the travel to China.

风景名胜

B: Yes, I've been longing to go to China for a long time.

A: So, have you had an idea about where to travel?

B: Definitely. I've always been **fascinated**① by traveling to the Great Wall. The Chinese people all say that he who does not reach the Great Wall is not a hero. So I think I must scale it.

A: Wow, that sounds great. Can you tell me more details?

B: Sure, it's my honor. The Great wall is the symbol of the Chinese nation. It took people over 2,000 years to complete. The most famous part of it are eight **precipitous**② passes. Also, there are some legendary beacon towers on it.

A: Well said. Can we travel to the Great Wall together?

B: Sure, I'm so glad. This will be a pleasant trip for us.

A: 我听说你在制订去中国旅游的计划。

B: 是的，我想去中国很久了。

A: 这么说，你已经决定去哪里旅游了？

B: 当然了。我一直对长城非常向往。中国人都说"不到长城非好汉"。所以，我一定要登一次长城。

A: 哇，听起来很棒。你能再多说一些吗？

B: 当然可以，这是我的荣幸。长城是中华民族的象征。人们耗时两千多年修建长城。长城险峻的八大关是最有名的。此外，长城上还有一些具有传奇色彩的烽火台。

A: 你说得太好了。我们能一起去长城旅游吗？

B: 当然能，我很乐意。这将是一次愉快的旅行。

生词注解 Notes

① span /spæn/ *vt.* 跨越；持续

② stretch /stretʃ/ *vi.* 延伸；伸展

③ miracle /ˈmɪrəkl/ *n.* 奇迹；奇迹般的人或物

④ architectural /ˌɑrkɪˈtektʃərəl/ *adj.* 建筑学的；建筑上的

⑤ strategic /strəˈtiːdʒɪk/ *adj.* 战略的；战略上的

⑥ vicissitude /vɪˈsɪsɪtjuːd/ *n.* 变迁；盛衰

⑦ wind /waɪnd/ *vt.* 弯曲前进；蜿蜒而行

⑧ heritage /ˈherɪtɪdʒ/ *n.* 遗产；传统

⑨ fascinate /ˈfæsɪneɪt/ *vt.* 使……着迷；使……神魂颠倒

⑩ precipitous /prɪˈsɪpɪtəs/ *adj.* 险峻的；急躁的

风景名胜

故宫

The Imperial Palace

导入语　Lead-in

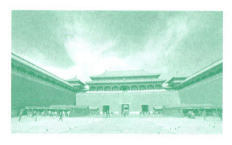

故宫，原名"紫禁城"，位于北京中轴线的中心，是世界上最大的皇家宫殿建筑群。故宫从1406年开始修建，到1420年最终建成，是世界上现存规模最大的宫殿型建筑，也是世界上最大的历史博物馆。从故宫建成到封建帝制结束，共有明清两代24位皇帝在此登基。故宫的建筑布局、形式和装饰等均体现了中国传统特色。故宫是国家5A级旅游景区、第一批全国重点文物保护单位、国家一级博物馆，1987年被联合国教科文组织列入《世界文化遗产名录》。

文化剪影　Cultural Outline

　　The Imperial Palace in Beijing is a **rectangle**①, the inner buildings are divided into the outer court and the inner court: the outer court center, composed of the Hall of **Supreme**② Harmony, the Hall of Central Harmony and the Hall of Preserving Harmony, is the place where the national grand ceremony was held; the inner court center, composed of the Palace of Heavenly Purity, the Hall of Union and Peace and the Palace of Earthly Tranquility, is the main palace where the emperors and empresses lived. The Imperical Palace is the largest and most complete ancient architectural complex in China, with a total area of more than 720,000 square meters. It is said that there're 9,999 and a half palaces, known as "The Sea of Palaces", which is an **unparalleled**③ masterpiece.

　　北京故宫呈长方形,其建筑分为外朝和内廷:外朝的中心由太和殿、中和殿、保和殿组成,是举行国家大典的地方;内廷的中心由乾清宫、交泰殿、坤宁宫组成,是皇帝和皇后居住的寝宫。故宫是中国现存最大、最完整的古建筑群,总面积72万多平方米,据说有殿宇宫室9999间半,被誉为"殿宇之海",堪称无与伦比的杰作。

　　The Hall of Supreme Harmony is the tallest building in the existing ancient Chinese architecture and the symbol of **feudal**④ imperial power. This is the place where the Ming and Qing emperors held a grand ceremony.

太和殿是中国现存古建筑中最高大的建筑,是封建皇权的象征。这里是明清两代皇帝举行大典的场所。

The building of the Imperial Palace takes the direction of north and south, setting up an **ornamental**⑤ column to determine its **orientation**⑥. In front of Tiananmen square, carved stone columns are used as an ornamental column to indicate the architectural direction of the entire Imperial Palace and to **coordinate**⑦ with the main architectural style.

故宫建筑坐北朝南,立华表以确定方位。天安门的石雕华表指示整座故宫的建筑方向,并与主体建筑风格相协调。

佳句点睛 Punchlines

1. The Imperial Palace is an outstanding example of the greatest **palatial**⑧ architecture complex in China.

故宫是中国最伟大的宫殿式建筑群的杰出代表。

2. The entire building of the Imperial Palace, beautifully decorated and magnificent, is known as one of the five major palaces in the world.

故宫的整体建筑装饰美丽,富丽堂皇,被誉为"世界五大宫殿"之一。

3. The last ray of the afterglow slants on the golden glazed tiles of the Imperial Palace, where a unique royal style emergs.

最后一抹余晖斜映在故宫的金色琉璃瓦上，呈现出特有的皇家风范。

 情景对话 Situational Dialogue

A: I've heard you're going to China next week.

B: Yes, that's the case. The other day, I read a magazine about the Imperial Palace. I cannot help myself stop visiting there.

A: The Imperial Palace of Ming and Qing was the royal residence from the 15th century to the early 20th century, and it was the state power center of the late feudal society in China.

B: There are countless masterpieces in the palace and each of them is unique and has their own culture.

A: I think it would be a **visual**① feast for people who visit them. The Imperial Palace is located at the center of Beijing's central axis. It is the largest imperial palace complex in the world and the largest history museum in the world.

B: You're right. It is really worth visiting.

A: I hope you have a good time.

B: Thank you.

A: 我听说你要去中国旅游了。

B: 是的,没错。前几天,我读了一本介绍故宫的杂志。我迫不及待地想去参观。

A: 明清故宫是15世纪至20世纪初的皇家居所,是中国封建社会晚期的国家权力中心。

B: 故宫里有数不清的杰作,每一件都是独一无二的,具有自己独特的文化。

A: 我想对于拜访参观的人来说,这一定是一场视觉盛宴。故宫位于北京中轴线的中心,是世界上最大的皇家宫殿建筑群,也是世界上最大的历史博物馆。

B: 说得对,故宫的确值得参观。

A: 希望你玩得愉快。

B: 谢谢你。

生词注解 Notes

① rectangle /ˈrektæŋgl/ *n.* 长方形;矩形

② supreme /suˈpriːm/ *adj.* 最高的;至高的

③ unparalleled /ʌnˈpærəleld/ *adj.* 无与伦比的;无双的

④ feudal /ˈfjuːdl/ *adj.* 封建制度的;领地的

⑤ ornamental /ˌɔːnəˈmentl/ *adj.* 装饰的;装饰性的

⑥ orientation /ˌɔːriːenˈteɪʃn/ *n.* 方向;定向

⑦ coordinate /kəʊˈɔːdɪneɪt/ *vi.* 协调;配合

⑧ palatial /pəˈleɪʃəl/ *adj.* 富丽堂皇的;宽敞的

⑨ visual /ˈvɪʒuəl/ *adj.* 视觉的;栩栩如生的

颐和园

The Summer Palace

  导入语 Lead-in

颐和园是皇家园林,其前身是清漪园,坐落于北京西郊,毗邻圆明园。颐和园以昆明湖、万寿山为基址,以杭州西湖为蓝本,既是汲取江南园林的精髓而建成的山水园林,也是保存最完整的皇家行宫御苑,被誉为"皇家园林博物馆"。颐和园占地面积达293公顷,主要由万寿山和昆明湖两部分组成,千姿百态的宫殿园林建筑三千余间,分为行政、生活和游览三部分。颐和园与承德避暑山庄、苏州拙政园和留园并称为"中国四大名园"。1998年,颐和园被联合国教科文组织列入《世界遗产名录》。

风景名胜

 文化剪影 Cultural Outline

The Summer Palace, which means "the garden of **nourishment**① and harmony" in Chinese, is the largest royal garden in China. The natural landscape of the hills and open water in the park is combined with **artificial**② shapes, harmonious and unified, and has an extremely high **aesthetic**③ value.

颐和园意为"颐养和谐之园",是中国最大的皇家园林,园内的丘陵和开阔水域由自然景观与人工景观构成,和谐统一,具有极高的审美价值。

The Summer Palace makes clever arrangements in the form of mountains and lakes, and borrows the scenery from the peaks of the Xishan Mountains. The buildings in the park absorb the **essence**④ of architecture from all over China, making the landscape in it varied and beautiful.

颐和园中的山湖布局巧妙,借景西山群峰,园内建筑吸收中国各地建筑的精华,使园内景色变幻无穷、美不胜收。

The Summer Palace is the royal court with the richest cultural **connotation**⑤, known as the "Royal Garden Museum". The eastern palace area and the inner court area are typical of the northern **quadrangles**⑥; the southern lake area is modeled after the West Lake in Hangzhou, a

West **Dike**[7] dividing the lake into two, with a strong **flavor**[8] of the southern Yangtze River; the northern part of the Longevity Hill is typical of the Tibetan lama temple style; and at Suzhou Street in the north there are shops in great numbers and crisscrossing waterways, which are also a typical water-bound-town style of the southern Yangtze River.

颐和园是文化内涵最丰富的皇家御苑,被誉为"皇家园林博物馆":东部的宫殿区和内廷区是典型的北方四合院风格;南部的湖泊区仿照杭州西湖景色,一道西堤把湖泊一分为二,具有浓郁的江南情调;万寿山的北面是典型的西藏喇嘛庙宇风格;北部的苏州街店铺林立,水道纵横,又是典型的江南水乡风格。

佳句点睛 Punchlines

1. The Summer Palace is the Chinese imperial garden of the Ming and Qing Dynasty, formerly known as the Qingyi Garden.

颐和园是中国明清时期皇家园林,前身为清漪园。

2. The Summer Palace covers a total area of 293 hectares, three-quarters of which is the water area.

颐和园总面积293公顷,其中四分之三是水域面积。

3. The Summer Palace is a great achievement of traditional gardening art, fully reflecting the principle of the classical Chinese garden that "although made by man, it seems to be created by nature".

风景名胜

颐和园集传统造园艺术之大成,充分体现了中国园林"虽由人作,宛自天开"的造园准则。

情景对话 Situational Dialogue

A: Oh, it is a really big garden and there is a lake inside.

B: Yes, the Summer Palace covers an area of 293 hectares. The whole project was known as the "three hills and the five gardens". It is your first visit at the Summer Palace, isn't it?

A: No, this is already my second. I guess if we look at the Summer Palace from a boat, it will offer a unique view.

B: The Kunming Lake in the center covers an area of 2.2 square kilometers and is completely dug by people. The **excavated**① soil is used to build the Longevity Hill. From a boat we can have a full view of the Longevity Hill. We can also row a boat across the Seventeen-arch Bridge.

A: I've heard that there're many shops on Suzhou Street.

B: Let's go there by boat.

A: 噢,这个花园可真不小,里面还有个湖。

B: 是的,颐和园占地293公顷,整个园林工程被称为"三山五园"。这是你第一次到颐和园吗?

A: 不,这已经是第二次了。我想,如果能从船上观看颐和园,一定会别有一番风味。

B: 中央的昆明湖占地2.2平方千米,完全由人工挖成,挖出的土被用来堆筑万寿山。在船上可以观看万寿山全景。我们还可以划小船穿过十七孔桥。

A: 我听说苏州街上店铺林立。

B: 咱们坐船到那里去吧。

生词注解　Notes

① nourishment /ˈnʌrɪʃmənt/　*n*. 营养品;滋养品

② artificial /ɑːtɪˈfɪʃl/　*adj*. 人造的;仿造的

③ aesthetic /ɛsˈθɛdɪk/　*adj*. 美学的;带来美感的

④ essence /ˈesns/　*n*. 精华;本质

⑤ connotation /kɑnəˈteɪʃ(ə)n/　*n*. 内涵;含义

⑥ quadrangle /ˈkwɑˌdræŋgəl/　*n*. 四方院;四边形

⑦ dyke /daɪk/　*n*. 堤坝

⑧ flavor /ˈfleɪvə(r)/　*n*. 情味;风味

⑨ excavate /ˈekskəveɪt/　*vt*. 挖掘;开凿

风景名胜

天坛

The Temple of Heaven

导入语 Lead-in

天坛始建于1420年,清朝乾隆和光绪年间曾经重修改建。天坛是明清皇帝祭天、祈谷的祭坛,有坛墙两重,形成内外坛。主要建筑在内坛,圜丘坛在南,祈谷坛在北,同在一条南北轴线上。坛内主要有祈年殿、皇乾殿、圜丘、皇穹宇等,还有回音壁、三音石、七星石等名胜古迹。天坛布局严谨,结构奇特,装饰瑰丽,是中国现存的精美古建筑群之一。天坛不仅是中国古建筑中的明珠,也是世界建筑史上的瑰宝。天坛是世界文化遗产、全国重点文物保护单位、国家5A级旅游景区和全国文明风景旅游区示范点。

文化剪影　Cultural Outline

Temples of various kinds are scattered in Beijing. The best-known are the Temple of Heaven in the south, the Temple of Earth in the north, the Temple of Sun in the east, and the Temple of the Moon in the west. The Temple of Heaven is the grandest of them all and also China's largest and best-preserved ancient temple **complex**①, which is the general name of the Hall of Prayer for Good Harvest and the **Circular**② Mound Altar, covering an area of about 2.73 million square meters on the east side of Yongdingmen Street in the southern part of Beijing City.

北京庙宇众多，南有天坛，北有地坛，东有日坛，西有月坛。天坛是其中最宏伟的一个，也是中国规模最大、保存最完整的古代祭天建筑群，是祈谷和圜丘的总称，位于北京市南部东城区永定门内大街东侧，占地约273万平方米。

In 1998, "Beijing Royal Altar—Temple of Heaven" was listed as *The World Cultural* **Heritage**③ *List* by UNESCO. The main design ideas of the Temple of Heaven **highlight**④ the vastness and height of the sky, expressing the **supremacy**⑤ of the "heaven", displaying the unique moral of the traditional Chinese culture.

1998年，"北京皇家祭坛——天坛"被联合国教科文组织列入《世界文化遗产名录》。天坛建筑的主要设计思想突出天空的辽阔高远，表现"天"的至高无上，同时也彰显出中国传统文化特有的寓意。

风景名胜

The Temple of Heaven's main building is the Hall of Prayer for Good Harvests, where emperors held annual ceremonies to worship the heaven to pray for good weather and **bumper**⑥ harvest. The Hall of Prayer for Good Harvests is a gilt triple-roofed round hall with blue **glazed**⑦ tiles as a symbol of heaven.

天坛的主体建筑是祈年殿，每年皇帝都在这里举行祭天仪式，祈祷风调雨顺、五谷丰登。祈年殿是一座鎏金宝顶三重檐圆形大殿，殿檐用蓝色琉璃瓦砌成，以此来象征天空。

佳句点睛 Punchlines

1. With lush trees and towering cypresses, the north-south axis of the Temple of Heaven and the **vicinity**⑧ of the complex provide a solemn backdrop to the altar.

天坛树木葱郁，南北轴线和建筑群附近古柏参天、树冠相接，把祭坛烘托得十分肃穆。

2. The structure of the Temple of Heaven is more complex than that of the Imperial Dome. The exterior is a three-story pavilion, and the interior is a dome-like structure that is layered and **looped**⑨, all of which are made of wood.

天坛的构造比皇穹宇复杂，外部是三层高阁，内部则是层层相叠而环接的穹顶式结构，全部采用木结构。

3. The echo wall of the Temple of Heaven is a circular wall. On one side, you can speak softly against the wall while on the other side you can hear clearly, just like making a phone call.

天坛的回音壁是一个圆形围墙，在一边贴着墙轻声说话，在另一边能听得一清二楚，就像打电话一样。

情景对话 Situational Dialogue

A: Welcome to the Temple of Heaven, which is the cultural heritage of China. Now we're gonna go along the route that leads to the altar. It will take roughly one hour. Mind you, the emperor also walked along this route to pay **tribute**⑩ to the god of heaven.

B: Wow, great. How big it is.

A: Yeah, the Temple of Heaven is much bigger than the Forbidden City and smaller than the Summer Palace with an area of about 2,700,000 square meters. As Chinese emperors called themselves "the son of heaven", they dared not to build their own dwelling "Forbidden City" bigger than the dwelling for heaven.

B: It's amazing that the Temple of Heaven has been preserved so well.

A: It has existed for more than 500 years since it was first built in 1420 in the Ming Dynasty to offer sacrifice to heaven.

B: No wonder millions of sightseers at home and abroad come to visit it every year.

风景名胜

A: Right. It's worth visiting. Let's go ahead.

B: OK, I can't wait to visit it.

A: 欢迎来到天坛,它是中国的文化遗产。现在我们沿路走向圣坛,大约需要一个小时。你们知道吗,皇帝也是走这条路去祭天。

B: 哇,太棒了,天坛好大啊!

A: 是啊,天坛的面积大约是270万平方米,比紫禁城大得多,比颐和园小。由于中国皇帝自称"天子",因此他们不敢把自己的居所紫禁城修建得比上天的祭坛大。

B: 天坛竟保存得如此完好。

A: 天坛始建于明代1420年,为祭天之用,到现在已有五百多年的历史了。

B: 难怪每年有国内外数百万的游客来天坛旅游。

A: 这里的确值得参观,让我们继续前进吧。

B: 好的,我都迫不及待了。

生词注解 Notes

① complex /ˈkɒmpleks/ n. 建筑群;综合设施

② circular /ˈsɜːkjələ(r)/ adj. 圆形的;循环的

③ heritage /ˈherɪtɪdʒ/ n. 遗产;传统

④ highlight /ˈhaɪlaɪt/ vt. 突出;强调

⑤ supremacy /suˈpreməsɪ/ n. 至高无上;主权

⑥ bumper /ˈbʌmpə(r)/ *adj.* 丰盛的;巨大的

⑦ glazed /gleɪzd/ *adj.* 上过釉的;呆滞无神的

⑧ vicinity /vəˈsɪnəti/ *n.* 邻近;附近

⑨ loop /luːp/ *vt.* 使……成环;环行

⑩ tribute /ˈtrɪbjuːt/ *n.* 称赞;敬意

风景名胜

避暑山庄

The Imperial Mountain Summer Resort

导入语 Lead-in

避暑山庄坐落于河北省承德市中心以北的狭长谷地上，环绕山庄的宫墙蜿蜒起伏长达万米，是中国现存最大的古典皇家园林。避暑山庄及其周边寺庙是一个紧密关联的有机整体，避暑山庄朴素淡雅，周边寺庙则金碧辉煌。避暑山庄是国家5A级旅游景区和全国重点文物保护单位。1961年，避暑山庄被定为第一批全国重点文物保护单位，与颐和园、拙政园、留园合称为"中国四大名园"。1994年，避暑山庄被联合国教科文组织列入《世界文化遗产名录》。

文化剪影　Cultural Outline

The Imperial Mountain Summer Resort is located in a narrow valley north of the city center of Chengde in Hebei Province and on the west bank of the Wulie River. With the style of simple but elegant mountain village and rustic appeal, it absorbs the scenery of natural landscape and becomes the largest ancient imperial palace in China. It is divided into palace area, lake area, plain area and mountain area, which is both a **microcosm**① of China's natural landscape and a glorious milestone in the history of Chinese gardens.

避暑山庄位于河北省承德市中心北部、武烈河西岸一带狭长的谷地上。避暑山庄以素雅的山村野趣为格调，取自然山水本色，成为中国现存占地最大的古代帝王宫苑。避暑山庄分为宫殿区、湖泊区、平原区和山峦区，既是中国自然地貌的缩影，也是中国园林史上一座辉煌的里程碑。

The Imperial Mountain Summer Resort was the place where the Qing emperors spent the summer and went hunting. It was also the place where Wushu **competitions**② were held and **ethnic**③ elites from all over the country were received. The emperors spent half of their time here every year.

避暑山庄是清朝皇帝避暑和狩猎的地方，也是常被用来举办武术比赛和接待全国各地少数民族精英的地方。皇帝每年有一半时间

风景名胜

要在这里度过。

The design of the Imeprial Mountain Summer Resort is outstanding because it has absorbed the design features of various garden styles, merged the features of water-bound villages in the south of the Yangtze River and the northern grasslands, and formed the **layout**① of the southeast lake district, the northwest mountain district and the northeast plain district.

避暑山庄之所以设计出色,是因为其吸纳了各种园林的设计风格,融汇了江南水乡和北方草原的特色,形成了东南湖区、西北山区和东北平原区的布局。

佳句点睛 Punchlines

1. The Imperial Mountain Summer Resort is one of the four most famous Chinese gardens and one of the well-preserved imperial palaces outside Beijing.

承德避暑山庄是中国四大名园,也是北京之外保存较好的帝王宫殿之一。

2. Jehol, the shortest river in the world, flows only 14.7 kilometers through the Mountain Summer Resort.

热河是世界上最短的河流,流经避暑山庄的部分只有14.7千米。

3. The Imperial Mountain Summer Resort and its **surrounding**⑤ temples were included in *The World Cultural Heritage List* in 1994.

1994年,避暑山庄及其周边庙宇被列入《世界文化遗产名录》。

情景对话　Situational Dialogue

A: Is the Imperial Mountain Summer Resort in Chengde a part of Beijing City?

B: No, it isn't. It is located in the city of Chengde in Northeastern Hebei Province.

A: How big is it?

B: It is the largest imperial garden in China and twice the size of the Summer Place in Beijing.

A: That is really large. It must take a very long time to have built it.

B: Definitely⑥. The whole building lasted 89 years, starting from Kangxi period in 1703 to Qianlong period in 1792.

A: I have to say it is a really waste of labor and money on such a huge garden, only for the emperors.

B: You're right. But it shows that the establishment of the Imperial Mountain Summer Resort achieved Emperor Kangxi's political goal of "combining the inner and outer hearts into a **consolidated**⑦ **undertaking**⑧".

风景名胜

A: 承德避暑山庄是北京的一部分吗?

B: 不是。承德避暑山庄位于河北省东北部的承德市。

A: 它有多大呢?

B: 它是中国最大的皇家园林,是北京颐和园的两倍大。

A: 那真的很大,一定花费了很长时间才建成吧?

B: 的确是。整个建筑从1703年康熙年间开始修建一直到1792年乾隆年间完成,耗时89年。

A: 不得不说,只是为了皇帝,建造这么大的花园真是浪费人力和物力。

B: 没错,但这同时也表明,避暑山庄的建立达到了康熙皇帝"合内外之心,成巩固之业"的政治目的。

生词注解 Notes

① microcosm /ˈmaɪkrəʊkɒzəm/ n. 微观世界;小宇宙

② competition /kɒmpəˈtɪʃn/ n. 竞争;竞赛

③ ethnic /ˈeθnɪk/ adj. 种族的;人种的

④ layout /ˈleɪaʊt/ n. 布局;设计

⑤ surrounding /səˈraʊndɪŋ/ adj. 周围的;附近的

⑥ definitely /ˈdefɪnətli/ adv. 肯定地;当然

⑦ consolidate /kənˈsɒlɪdeɪt/ vt. 巩固;加强

⑧ undertaking /ˌʌndəˈteɪkɪŋ/ n. 事业;企业

孔庙、孔府和孔林

The Confucian Temple, Mansion and Graveyard

  导入语 Lead-in

　　孔子是中国春秋末期著名的思想家和教育家,被尊为儒家学派的创始人。他创立的儒学思想在中国乃至世界历史上都具有重大影响。孔庙、孔府和孔林位于山东曲阜,是中国唯一集祭祀孔子嫡系后裔的府邸和孔子及其子孙墓地于一体、规模最大的建筑群。孔庙、孔府和孔林的历史价值、科学价值与艺术价值集中体现在其保存完好的文物上,30万件孔府明清文书档案是中国最丰富的私家档案,也是研究明清历史的重要资料。1994年,孔庙、孔府和孔林被联合国教科文组织列入《世界文化遗产名录》。

风景名胜

文化剪影　Cultural Outline

The Confucian Temple, built in the 478 BC, is in the heartland of Qufu City, Shandong Province. The Confucian **Mansion**①, next to the temple, is the home of the Confucian **descendants**②, second only to the Imperial Palace in size. The Confucian Graveyard is located on the outskirts of the north of the Confucian Mansion while it is also the largest man-made **mausoleum**③ and the oldest and most complete clan cemetery in China.

孔庙位于山东省曲阜市中心，建于前478年。孔府紧邻孔庙，是孔子后裔居住的地方，规模仅次于故宫。孔林位于孔府以北城郊，是中国最大的人造陵园，也是保存年代最长、最完整的氏族古墓园。

The Confucian Temple, also known as the "Most Sacred Temple", is a place to worship Confucius, his wife and his seventy-two **sages**④. The Confucian Temple, along with Beijing's Imperial Palace and Hebei's Imperial Mountain Summer Resort, is known as "China's three architectural **complexes**⑤".

孔庙，又称"至圣庙"，是祭祀孔子及其夫人和七十二贤人的地方。孔庙与北京故宫、河北承德避暑山庄并称"中国三大古建筑群"。

The Confucian Graveyard, also known as the "Most Sacred Graveyard", is located 1.5 kilometers north of Qufu City, Shandong Province.

It is the family cemetery of Confucius and his descendants, and the world's longest lasting family cemetery. There are now more than 100,000 trees in the graveyard.

孔林,也称"至圣林",位于山东省曲阜市城北1.5千米处,是孔子及其后裔的家族墓地,也是世界上延续时间最长的家族墓地。目前,孔林内已有10万多棵各种树木。

佳句点睛 Punchlines

1. Confucius's historical role in shaping China's national character and traditional culture has been **unmatched**⑥ for 2,000 years.

孔子在塑造中国民族性格和传统文化上的历史地位,两千年来无人可及。

2. The Confucian Temple has a long history, a large scale and a complete preservation, which is rare in the world.

孔庙建筑时间久远,规模宏大,保存完整,世所罕见。

3. The Confucian Graveyard is located on the outskirts of the north of the Confucian Mansion. With a **circumference**⑦ of more than ten kilometers, it is the largest man-made cemetery in China.

孔林位于孔府以北的城郊,周长十几千米,是中国最大的一座人造陵园。

风景名胜

情景对话　Situational Dialogue

A: I've learnt about Confucius in school. It's amazing that most of his ideas still hold true today.

B: Yeah, I have that class, too. He is one of the famous and the great philosophers in the world.

A: I agree with you. Qufu is the hometown of Confucius, a great thinker, educator and statesman in ancient China.

B: Yeah, I have learnt from the book about the Confucian Temple, Mansion and Graveyard.

A: The Confucian Temple, built in 478 BC, is in the center of Qufu City. There are 466 buildings in the temple, covering a total area of 21.8 hectares. Dozens of **renovations**[8] and **expansions**[9] have made the Confucian Temple a large-scale ancient building complex with nine rows of courtyards.

B: Why don't we go to visit it? It's really worth touring.

A: That sounds like a good idea.

B: Let's go together then.

A: 我在学校里学习了有关孔子的思想。孔子的大部分思想在今天仍然适用,真让人惊讶。

B: 嗯,我也上过那门课。孔子是世界上著名的伟大思想家之一。

A: 我同意你的看法。曲阜是我国古代伟大的思想家、教育家、政治家孔子的故里。

B: 是的，我从书上了解到了孔庙、孔府和孔林。

A: 孔庙位于曲阜市中心，建于前478年。庙里有466间各式建筑，总面积约21.8公顷。孔庙经过数十次重修和扩建，成为拥有九进院落、规模宏大的古建筑群。

B: 我们何不去那里看看呢？这值得好好参观一下。

A: 听起来是个好主意。

B: 那咱们一块去吧。

生词注解　Notes

① mansion /ˈmænʃn/　n. 宅邸；大厦

② descendant /dɪˈsendənt/　n. 后代；弟子

③ mausoleum /ˌmɔːzəˈliːəm/　n. 大型陵墓；阴森森的大厦

④ sage /seɪdʒ/　n. 圣人；贤人

⑤ complex /ˈkɒmpleks/　n. 建筑群；综合设施

⑥ unmatched /ˌʌnˈmætʃt/　adj. 无与伦比的；无匹敌的

⑦ circumference /səˈkʌmfərəns/　n. 圆周；周长

⑧ renovation /ˌrenəˈveɪʃn/　n. 翻修；整修

⑨ expansion /ɪkˈspænʃn/　n. 扩张；扩展

苏州古典园林

Suzhou Classical Gardens

 导入语 Lead-in

苏州古典园林是江苏省苏州市山水园林建筑的统称,又称"苏州园林",以私家园林为主,目前保存完整的有60多处,对外开放的园林有19处。苏州园林是中华园林文化的佼佼者,主要有沧浪亭、狮子林、拙政园、留园、怡园等。苏州园林是国家5A级旅游景区、中国十大风景名胜之一。苏州素有"园林之城"的美誉,享有"江南园林甲天下,苏州园林甲江南"的盛誉。1997年,苏州古典园林作为中国园林的代表被联合国教科文组织列入《世界文化遗产名录》。

文化剪影　Cultural Outline

Suzhou Classical Gardens is the representative of the essence of gardens at the south of the Yangtze River, displaying many different styles of gardens in the Yuan, Ming and Qing dynasties. Canglang Pavilion, Lion Forest, **Humble**① Administrator's Garden and Lingering Garden are the four famous gardens in Suzhou. In 1997, Suzhou Classical Garden was included in *The World Heritage List* by UNESCO.

苏州古典园林是江南园林精髓的代表，展示了许多元、明、清代不同风格的园林。沧浪亭、狮子林、拙政园和留园是苏州四大名园。1997年，苏州古典园林被联合国教科文组织列入《世界文化遗产名录》。

Suzhou Classical Gardens have their own characteristics in terms of layout, structure and style. They are the "**urban**② mountain forests" full of natural charm in the city. People can enjoy the natural "landscape forests and springs" when they enter the gardens.

苏州古典园林在布局、结构和风格上自成一派，是城市中充满自然意趣的"城市山林"，进入园林，人们便可享受到大自然的"山水林泉之乐"。

Suzhou Classical Gardens are the literati freehand landscape ones with profound cultural significance. Most of the Suzhou gardens are lit-

145

tle and **dainty**③, making people feel as if they are in the painting. The Suzhou Classical Gardens is like a shining pearl, which is a brilliant **component**④ of contemporary Chinese cultural heritage.

苏州古典园林是文化意蕴深厚的文人写意山水园。苏州园林大多小巧玲珑，置身其中让人有身在画中的感觉。苏州古典园林就像一颗明珠，是当代中国文化遗产一个辉煌的组成部分。

 佳句点睛 Punchlines

1. Suzhou Classical Gardens are not only a product of Chinese history and culture, but also a carrier of traditional Chinese ideology and culture.

苏州古典园林不仅是历史文化的产物，也是中国传统思想文化的载体。

2. In the Song Dynasty, there was the saying that "Suzhou on earth matches paradise in Heaven" and "**bumper**⑤ harvests in Suzhou alone are enough for the whole nation".

宋代就有"上有天堂，下有苏杭"和"苏湖熟，天下足"的说法。

3. Located in in Sanyuanfang, south of Suzhou City, Canglang Pavilion has the longest history among the existing gardens in Suzhou. Its natural and harmonious layout is a masterpiece of **ingenious**⑥ design and **appropriate**⑦ technique.

沧浪亭位于苏州城南三元坊,在现存的苏州园林中历史最为悠久,全园布局自然和谐,堪称构思巧妙、手法得当的杰作。

情景对话 Situational Dialogue

A: I've heard an old saying that "the gardens south of the Yangtze River are the best on earth, and among them the gardens of Suzhou are the best".

B: Yes, Suzhou Classical Gardens are the most outstanding representatives of Chinese classical gardens.

A: Are there many gardens in Suzhou?

B: Yes, there are. The gardens first appeared in the Spring and Autumn Period, developed in the Song and Yuan dynasties, and **flourished**① in the Ming and Qing dynasties. By the late Qing Dynasty, Suzhou had over 170 gardens of **diverse**② styles, which earned it the title of "The City of Gardens". At present, there are more than 60 well-preserved gardens and more than 10 open to the public. The Surging Wave Pavilion, the Lion Grove, the Humble Administrator's Garden and the Lingering Garden are known as the four most famous gardens in Suzhou **respectively**③ representing the artistic styles of the Song, Yuan, Ming and Qing dynasties.

A: I think they must be extremely beautiful.

B: Definitely, Suzhou is a "Paradise on Earth".

风景名胜

A: 我听说,"江南园林甲天下,苏州园林甲江南"。

B: 是的,苏州园林是中国古典园林最杰出的代表。

A: 苏州有很多园林吗?

B: 是的,苏州园林始于春秋,兴于宋元,盛于明清。清末苏州已有各色园林170余处,为其赢得了"园林之城"的美誉。目前苏州保存完好的园林有60多处,对外开放的有10多处。其中沧浪亭、狮子林、拙政园和留园分别代表了宋、元、明、清四个朝代的艺术风格,被称为"苏州四大名园"。

A: 我想它们肯定很漂亮。

B: 当然,苏州可是"人间天堂"。

生词注解　Notes

① humble /ˈhʌmbl/　*adj.* 谦卑的;谦逊的

② urban /ˈɜːbən/　*adj.* 城市的;住在都市的

③ dainty /ˈdeɪnti/　*adj.* 秀丽的;讲究的

④ component /kəmˈpəʊnənt/　*n.* 组成部分;成分

⑤ bumper /ˈbʌmpə(r)/　*adj.* 巨大的;丰盛的

⑥ ingenious /ɪnˈdʒiːniəs/　*adj.* 有独创性的;机灵的

⑦ appropriate /əˈprəʊpriət/　*adj.* 适当的;恰当的

⑧ flourish /ˈflʌrɪʃ/　*vi.* 繁荣;茁壮成长

⑨ diverse /daɪˈvɜːs/　*adj.* 多种多样的;形形色色的

⑩ respectively /rɪˈspektɪvlɪ/　*adv.* 分别地;各自地

武当山古建筑群

The Ancient Building Complex in Mount Wudang

 导入语 Lead-in

武当山古建筑群建于唐贞观年间,明代达到鼎盛,主要有太和拱、南岩宫、紫云宫、复真观和石坊等,形成了"五里一庵十里宫,丹墙翠瓦望玲珑"的完美格局,绵延起伏70千米,堪称中国古代建筑史上的一大奇观,被誉为"中国古代建筑成就的博物馆"和"挂在悬崖峭壁上的故宫"。武当山是第一批全国重点风景名胜区、国家5A级风景区、道教圣地和武当武术发源地,被誉为"天下第一仙山"。1994年,武当山古建筑群被联合国教科文组织列入《世界文化遗产名录》。

文化剪影 Cultural Outline

The ancient building complex in Mount Wudang is located in Shiyan City, Hubei Province, with the Golden Palace on the Tianzhu Peak as the center, and the official road and ancient Shendao (tomb passage) as the axis, the heritage reserve covering an area of 15,000 hectares and the **buffer**① zone of 800 hectares.

武当山古建筑群位于湖北省十堰市境内,以天柱峰金殿为中心,以官道和古神道为轴线向四周辐射,遗产保护区面积15000公顷,缓冲区800公顷。

Mount Wudang is located in Danjiangkou, Shiyan City, Hubei Province, **bordering**② Xiangyang City in the east, Shiyan City in the west, Shennongjia in the south and Danjiangkou Reservoir in the north. The mount is unique in its features, which boasts of the majesty of Mount Tai and the steepness of Mount Hua, as well as deep streams, clear springs, **secluded**③ caves and cliffs.

武当山位于湖北省十堰市丹江口境内,东接襄阳市,西靠十堰市,南依神农架,北临丹江口水库,山势奇特,既有泰山的雄峻,又有华山的奇险,更有深涧、清泉、幽洞和悬崖。

The ancient building complex in Mount Wudang is based on the traditional Chinese Fengshui Theory. From Jingle Palace to Tianzhu

Peak, the Royal Family built 33 groups of large building complexes, paying particular attention to keeping in harmony with the **environment**① in **orientation**⑤, spacing, volume and color, like fairyland on earth.

武当山古建筑群根据中国传统风水理论修建,从净乐宫到天柱峰,皇家共建有33组大建筑群,在朝向、间距、体量和色彩上尤其注重与环境保持协调一致,犹如人间仙境。

佳句点睛 Punchlines

1. Mount Wudang has a long history of Taoist culture and is a famous Taoist holy land, **ranking**⑥ first among the four famous Taoist mountains.

武当山道教文化源远流长,是著名的道教圣地,位居道教四大名山之首。

2. The ancient architectural complex of Mount Wudang embodies the Taoist idea of "respecting nature" and maintains the natural **primitive**⑦ style of Mount Wudang.

武当山古建筑群体现了道教"崇尚自然"的思想,保留了武当山的自然原始风貌。

3. The ancient building complexes of Mount Wudang are rich in ancient Chinese science and technology and cultural **connotation**⑧,

which shows the wisdom and artistic creativity of the ancient Chinese working people.

武当山古建筑群具有丰富的中国古代科技与文化内涵,彰显了古代中国劳动人民的聪明才智与艺术创意。

 情景对话　Situational Dialogue

A: What do you prefer to do on vacation?

B: I prefer to visit famous scenic spots.

A: Where do you plan to travel this winter vacation?

B: I plan to visit the Mount Wudang in Hubei Province.

A: I know Wudang, which is the center of Taoism.

B: Right. The Gold Hall, built high on the top of the Tianzhu Peak in 1416, is the largest copper structure existing in China, which makes people realize the mystery and magic of Taoism's "**unity**① of nature and man" and "following the course of nature".

A: The entire building complex is centered on the Golden **Dome**② and the eight palaces as the main body, with the style of royal religious architecture.

B: That's right. So I wanna see it with my own eyes.

A: 你在假期喜欢做什么?

B: 我喜欢参观一些著名景点。

A: 你这个寒假打算去哪里旅游?

B: 我打算去湖北的武当山。

A: 我知道武当,它是道教的中心。

B: 没错。建于1416年的金殿高高地耸立在天柱峰顶,它是我国现存最大的铜质建筑,让人体会到道家"天人合一"和"道法自然"的玄妙与神奇。

A: 整个建筑群以金顶为中心,八大宫为主体,具有皇家宗教建筑的气派。

B: 的确如此,所以我想亲眼去看一看。

生词注解 Notes

① buffer /ˈbʌfə(r)/ n. 缓冲物;缓冲区

② border /ˈbɔːdə(r)/ vi. 接界;接壤

③ secluded /sɪˈkluːdɪd/ adj. 僻静的;幽静的

④ environment /ɪnˈvaɪrənmənt/ n. 生存环境;自然环境

⑤ orientation /ˌɔːriənˈteɪʃn/ n. 取向;定向

⑥ rank /ræŋk/ vi. 排列;把……等分

⑦ primitive /ˈprɪmətɪv/ adj. 原始的;远古的

⑧ connotation /ˌkɒnəˈteɪʃn/ n. 内涵;含蓄

⑨ unity /ˈjuːnəti/ n. 统一;团结

⑩ dome /dəʊm/ n. 穹顶;圆顶状物

云冈石窟

The Yungang Grottoes

导入语 Lead-in

云冈石窟位于山西省大同市西郊16千米处,在武州山南麓、武州川北岸。整个石窟依山开凿,规模宏大,雕技精湛,栩栩如生,是5世纪中西文化融合的历史丰碑,被誉为中国古代雕刻艺术的宝库,是石窟艺术"中国化"的开始。云冈石窟是中国大规模的古代石窟群之一,与敦煌莫高窟、洛阳龙门石窟和麦积山石窟并称为"中国四大石窟艺术宝库"。1961年,云冈石窟被国务院公布为全国首批重点文物保护单位。2001年,被联合国教科文组织列入《世界文化遗产名录》。2007年,被国家旅游局评为首批国家5A级旅游景区。

文化剪影 Cultural Outline

The Yungang Grottoes, one of the large ancient grottoes in China, is located at the southern foot of the Wuzhou Mountain, 16 kilometers west of Datong City, Shanxi Province. It was **excavated**① in the Northern Wei Dynasty in the middle of the fifth century. The grottoes were **hewn**② against the mountain, where there are 45 main caverns, more than 209 attached caves, more than 1,100 **niches**③ for the statues of Buddha, more than 59,000 large or small statues, and more than 18,000 square meters of sculpture area.

云冈石窟是中国大规模的古代石窟群之一，位于山西省大同市西郊16千米处的武州山南麓，开凿于5世纪中叶的北魏时期。石窟依山开凿，现存有主要洞窟45个，附属洞窟209个，佛龛1100多个，大小造像59000多尊，雕刻面积达18000余平方米。

The Yungang Grottoes were known as "Wuzhou Mountain Grotto Temple" or "Lingyan Temple" during the Northern Wei Dynasty. It not only represents the highest level of stone carving art in northern China in the fifth century, but is also called "the Northern Wei Dynasty carved on the stone".

云冈石窟在北魏时期被称为"武州山石窟寺"或"灵岩寺"，其不仅代表了5世纪中国北方石雕艺术的最高水平，也被称为"刻在石头上的北魏王朝"。

风景名胜

The entire grotto is large in scale, rich in imagery, colorful in pose, superb in carving, and vivid in image creation. All the Buddha statues here are adopted with the superb technique of **personification**④ and with vivid expression and boundless **vitality**⑤, which is worth the ancient treasure of Chinese civilization.

整个石窟规模宏大、造像丰富、形态各异、雕技精湛、栩栩如生。这里所有的佛像都采用拟人的高超手法,表情生动,活力无限,不愧为中华文明的古老珍宝。

佳句点睛 Punchlines

1. The large open-air Buddha in Cavern 20 looks solemn and **vigorous**⑥, known as the symbol of the Yungang Grottoes.

第二十窟的露天大佛神情肃穆,刚健雄浑,被誉为云冈石窟的象征。

2. The Yungang Grottoes is a historical **monument**⑦ left by the Xianbei Dynasty of the Northern Wei when the capital Pingcheng (now Datong, Shanxi) was built.

云冈石窟是北魏鲜卑王朝建都平城(今山西大同)时留下的一座历史丰碑。

3. The Yungang Grottoes vividly records the historical **trajectory**⑧ of the development from the Indian and Central Asian

Buddhist art to the Chinese Buddhist art.

云冈石窟形象地记录了印度及中亚佛教艺术向中国佛教艺术发展的历史轨迹。

 情景对话 **Situational Dialogue**

A: Have you ever heard about the Yungang Grottoes?

B: Of course, I have. The Yungang Grottoes and the Mogao Grottoes, the Longmen Grottoes and the Maijishan Grottoes are collectively known as the "Four Great Grottoes in China".

A: I toured there last week.

B: So what impressed you most?

A: The central sitting statue of the third Buddha is the largest Buddha statue in the fifth grotto. It is **demure**① but has the characteristics of the foreign Buddhism culture.

B: Oh, I got it. But I heard the sixth cavern is the most representative in the Yungang Grottoes. The wall is carved with the story of Sakyamuni from birth to Buddhahood.

A: Oh. In the middle of the cavern, there are two floors up to fifteen meters high. There are statues on every side of the floor, surrounded by statues of Buddha, **Bodhisattvas**② and Apsaras.

B: That sounds pretty vivid.

A: 你听过云冈石窟吗?

风景名胜

B:当然,云冈石窟与莫高窟、龙门石窟和麦积山石窟被合称为"中国四大石窟"。

A:我上周去那里旅游了。

B:你印象最深刻的是什么?

A:第五石窟中三世佛的中央坐像是石窟中最大的佛像。佛像形态端庄,具有外域佛教文化的特征。

B:噢,我明白了。但是,我听说第六石窟是云冈石窟中最具代表性的洞窟,壁上雕刻有释迦牟尼从诞生到成佛的故事。

A:噢,第六窟中央有连接窟顶的两层高达十五米的塔柱。每层四面都雕有塑像,周围雕满了佛、菩萨和飞天的造像。

B:听起来蛮生动的。

生词注解 Notes

① excavate /ˈekskəveɪt/ vt. 挖掘;开凿

② hew /hju:/ vt. 镂刻;砍伐

③ niche /ni:ʃ/ n. 壁龛;合适的职业

④ personification /pəˌsɒnɪfɪˈkeɪʃn/ n. 人格化;化身

⑤ vitality /vaɪˈtæləti/ n. 活力;生命力

⑥ vigorous /ˈvɪɡərəs/ adj. 有力的;精力充沛的

⑦ monument /ˈmɒnjumənt/ n. 纪念碑;不朽的作品

⑧ trajectory /trəˈdʒektəri/ n. 轨迹;抛物线

⑨ demure /dɪˈmjʊə(r)/ adj. 端庄的;严肃的

⑩ Bodhisattvas /ˌbɒdɪˈsɑ:tvəs/ n.(佛教中的)菩萨

秦始皇陵及兵马俑

The Mausoleum of the First Emperor of Qin and Terracotta Warriors

 导入语　Lead-in

秦始皇陵及兵马俑，又称"秦陵兵马俑"，位于陕西省西安市，被称为"世界第八大奇迹"。秦始皇陵，也称"骊山陵"，建于前246年至前208年，历时39年，是秦始皇的陵墓，也是中国第一个规模宏大、布局讲究、保存完好的帝王陵园。秦陵陵基近覆斗方形，夯土筑成，陵基东西宽345米，南北长350米。兵马俑是秦始皇陵的陪葬坑，位于秦始皇陵封土以东大约1.5千米处。秦始皇陵及兵马俑是中国第一批世界文化遗产、第一批全国重点文物保护单位、第一批国家5A级旅游景区，1987年被联合国教科文组织列入《世界文化遗产名录》。古埃及金字塔是世界上最大的地上王陵,中国的秦始皇陵则是世界上最大的地下皇陵。

文化剪影　Cultural Outline

The **Mausoleum**① of the First Emperor of Qin is the first imperial tomb with a grand scale, decent layout and well preserved in Chinese history. The Mausoleum of the First Emperor of Qin has not yet been **excavated**②. But his Terracotta Warriors unearthed near the mausoleum have been known as "The Eighth Wonder of the World" and are the largest pottery **figurine**③ group ever unearthed in China.

秦始皇陵是中国秦朝皇帝秦始皇的陵墓,也是中国第一个规模宏大、布局讲究、保存完好的帝王陵寝。秦始皇的陵墓还未被挖掘。但是,陵墓附近出土的兵马俑已被誉为"世界第八大奇迹",是中国已经出土的最大陶俑群。

The Terracotta Warriors is made up of three pits, with a total area of nearly twenty thousand square meters. The terracotta warriors and horses were **arrayed**④ according to the battle formation of the Qin Dynasty, symbolizing the troops keeping **vigil**⑤ beside the mausoleum and **demonstrating**⑥ a powerful military array under the rule of the First Emperor of Qin.

秦始皇兵马俑由三个俑坑组成,总面积近两万平方米。兵马俑按照秦朝的战斗队形排列,象征着军队在陵墓旁守夜,展示了秦始皇统领下的强大军事列阵。

As the world's largest underground military museum, the Terracotta Warriors of the First Emperor of Qin are well laid out with an unusual structure and with the east-west load-bearing walls set up at intervals of three meters at the bottom of the pit, about five meters deep, to separate the orderly rows of soldiers.

秦始皇兵马俑是世界上最大的地下军事博物馆,俑坑布局合理,结构奇特,在深五米左右的坑底每隔三米架起一道东西向的承重墙,隔开整齐排列的战士。

佳句点睛　Punchlines

1. The Mausoleum of the First Emperor of Qin is the largest imperial tomb of ancient China.

秦始皇陵墓是中国古代最大的帝王陵寝。

2. Terracotta Wariors have individual features and facial expressions, line up in battle-readiness, creating an **awe-inspiring**[①] effect.

兵马俑形象各异,千姿百态,按备战列队,营造出令人畏惧的效果。

3. The vast group of Terracotta Warriors buried in the pits is the **epitome**[②] of the powerful army of the Qin Dynasty.

风景名胜

兵马俑中埋藏的浩大俑群是秦王朝强大军队的缩影。

情景对话　Situational Dialogue

A: It's my first time to Xi'an. I know it is your hometown. Can you please be my free tour guide?

B: It's my honor.

A: Look, is this the Terracotta Warriors Museum?

B: Yes, let's go to take a look.

A: It's really big. There are so many exhibition halls. Which one should we go first?

B: Let's start with the first pit. It is the first exhibition hall opened to public.

A: Wow, how **spectacular**①! So many terracotta figures. Is this the Mausoleum of the First Emperor of Qin?

B: No, it isn't. Due to the technical problem, the Mausoleum of the First Emperor of Qin has not been excavated. We have just opened up the funerary objects—the Terracotta Warriors.

A: What a pity! The Mausoleum of the First Emperor of Qin was constructed over 38 years, facing Weishui River in the north and close to the tourist resort Huaqing Hot Spring in the west. I do wanna visit it.

B: Don't be sad. I believe we will see it in future.

A: 这是我第一次来西安。我知道西安是你的故乡,你能当我的免费导游吗?

B: 这是我的荣幸。

A: 这是兵马俑博物馆吗?

B: 是的,我们一起去看看。

A: 真大,这里有很多展厅,我们先去哪一个呢?

B: 先从第一个坑开始看吧,这是第一个向公众开放的展厅。

A: 哇,多么壮观! 这里就是秦始皇陵了吧?

B: 不是。由于科学技术的缘故,秦始皇陵还不能打开,我们只挖掘了其陪葬品——兵马俑。

A: 多么可惜啊! 据说,秦始皇陵北面朝渭河,西面接近华清池,修建时间长达38年。我真的好想参观啊。

B: 不要难过,我相信以后会有机会看到的。

生词注解　Notes

① mausoleum /mɔːzəˈliːəm/　n. 陵墓;阴森森的大厦

② excavate /ˈekskəveɪt/　vt. 发掘(古物);挖掘

③ figurine /fɪɡəˈriːn/　n. 小雕像;小塑像

④ array /əˈreɪ/　vt. 排列;列阵

⑤ vigil /ˈvɪdʒɪl/　n. 值夜;守夜祈祷

⑥ demonstrate /ˈdemənstreɪt/　vt. 展示;证明

⑦ awe-inspiring /ˈɔː ɪnspaɪərɪŋ/　adj. 令人敬畏的;使人畏惧的

⑧ epitome /ɪˈpɪtəmɪ/　n. 缩影;典型的人或事物

⑨ spectacular /spekˈtækjələ(r)/　adj. 壮观的;引人入胜的

风景名胜

少林寺

Shaolin Temple

导入语 Lead-in

少林寺，位于河南省登封市西北少室山五乳峰下，被誉为"天下第一名刹"。少林寺是佛教禅宗的祖庭，少林功夫的要旨是禅武合一，经历代少林武僧潜心研创并不断发扬光大，素有"天下功夫出少林，少林功夫甲天下"的美誉。少林功夫是中国武术中体系最庞大的门派，"少林"已经成为中国传统武术的象征。少林寺是全国重点文物保护单位、国家5A级旅游景区。2010年，包括少林寺常住院、初祖庵和塔林在内的"天地之中"历史建筑群被联合国教科文组织列入《世界文化遗产名录》。

文化剪影　Cultural Outline

Located at the western foot of Mount Song, southwest of Zhengzhou, Henan Province, Shaolin Temple is an important Buddhist **shrine**① as well as a training center for Chinese Gongfu. Shaolin Gongfu is the biggest school of Chinese Wushu, while "Shaolin" has become the symbol of Chinese traditional Wushu.

少林寺坐落在河南省郑州市西南嵩山西麓,它不仅是重要的佛教圣地,也是中国功夫的训练中心。少林功夫是中国武术中体系最庞大的门派,"少林"已经成为中国传统武术的象征。

Shaolin Temple is well known not only for its ancient and mysterious Buddhist culture, but also for its superb Shaolin Gongfu. "The Chinese Wushu crowns the world, the world Wushu out of Shaolin." Here is the birthplace of Shaolin Wushu, which is also **universally**② recognized as the **authentic**③ school of Chinese Wushu.

少林寺不仅因古老神秘的佛教文化,更因精湛的少林功夫而名扬天下。"中国功夫冠天下,天下功夫出少林",这里是少林武术的发源地,少林武术也是举世公认的中国武术正宗流派。

Shaolin Temple is the birthplace of Chinese Zen. "Zen" and "Wu" are two characteristics of Shaolin Temple. Zen **Buddhism**④ is an important **sect**⑤ in Buddhism, which is formed by the **fusion**⑥ of

Chinese native religion and part of **Confucianism**⁷, and has a far-reaching influence on Chinese culture.

少林寺是中国禅宗的发源地。"禅"和"武"是少林寺的两大特征。禅宗是佛教中的一个重要派别，它融合了中国本土的宗教和儒家思想的一部分内容，对中国文化有深远的影响。

佳句点睛　Punchlines

1. Because it is located in the dense **jungle**⁸ of Mount Shaoshi in the hinterland of Mount Song, it was named "Shaolin Temple".

因坐落于嵩山腹地少室山的茂密丛林之中，故名"少林寺"。

2. Shaolin Temple is the birthplace of Chinese Zen Buddhism Temple and Chinese Gongfu.

少林寺是中国佛教禅宗祖庭和中国功夫的发源地。

3. Shaolin Temple is one of the world cultural heritages and of the national key cultural relic protection units.

少林寺是世界文化遗产和全国重点文物保护单位。

情景对话　Situational Dialogue

A: Welcome to Henan.

B: I just have three days to stay in Henan. I wanna enjoy a great trip here.

A: I'll make full use of time to let you visit more places in your stay.

B: Can you introduce something about Shaolin Temple? I saw the movie *Shaolin Temple* years ago, which has impressed me deeply.

A: Sure, Shaolin Temple was built in 495. It was named because it is hidden deep in the dense forest of Mount Shaoshi.

B: Anything else?

A: Also, Shaolin Wushu is recognized as one of the authentic **martial**① arts while Zen and Chinese Gongfu are two features of Shaolin Temple.

B: Sounds I'm about to **embark on**② a magical journey.

A: 欢迎来到河南。

B: 我在河南只待三天,希望有一段快乐的旅途。

A: 我会充分利用时间让你参观更多的地方。

B: 你能给我介绍一下少林寺吗?我很多年前就看过《少林寺》,这部电影给我留下了深刻的印象。

A: 当然能,少林寺建于495年,因它隐藏在少室山的密林深处而得名。

B: 还有呢?

A: 还有就是,少林武术是被公认的正宗武术流派之一,"禅"和"武"是少林寺的两大特征。

B: 听起来我即将开启一段神奇之旅喽。

生词注解 Notes

① shrine /ʃraɪn/   *n.* 圣殿；圣地

② universally /ˌjuːnɪˈvɜːsəli/   *adv.* 普遍地；广泛地

③ authentic /ɔːˈθentɪk/   *adj.* 真正的；正宗的

④ Buddhism /ˈbʊdɪzəm/   *n.* 佛教；佛门

⑤ sect /sekt/   *n.* 流派；宗派

⑥ fusion /ˈfjuːʒn/   *n.* 融合；熔化

⑦ Confucianism /kənˈfjuːʃənɪzəm/   *n.* 儒教；儒家思想

⑧ jungle /ˈdʒʌŋgl/   *n.* 丛林；密林

⑨ martial /ˈmɑːʃl/   *adj.* 尚武的；军事的

⑩ embark /ɪmˈbɑːk/ on   开始；着手

龙门石窟

The Longmen Grottoes

 导入语 Lead-in

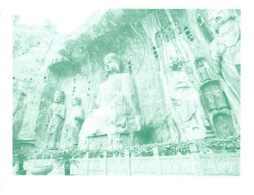

龙门石窟，别称"伊阙"，位于河南省洛阳市洛龙区伊河两岸的龙门山与香山上，开凿于北魏孝文帝年间，历经东魏、西魏、北齐、隋、唐、五代、宋等朝代连续、大规模营造达四百余年之久。石窟南北长达1000米，现存窟龛2345个，造像10万余尊，碑刻题记2800余件，堪称大型石刻艺术博物馆，代表了中国石刻艺术的最高峰，其中"龙门二十品"是书法魏碑的精华，褚遂良所书的"伊阙佛龛之碑"是初唐楷书艺术的典范。龙门石窟是全国重点文物保护单位和中国石刻艺术宝库之一，也是国家5A级旅游景区，2000年被联合国教科文组织列入《世界文化遗产名录》。

文化剪影　Cultural Outline

The Longmen Grottoes is located in Luoyang City, Henan Province. These grottoes were excavated during the period of Emperor Xiaowen of the Northern Wei Dynasty and had continued for more than 400 years until the Northern Song Dynasty. It is the three treasure **troves**① of ancient Chinese Buddhist grotto art, along with the Mogao Grottoes in Dunhuang, Gansu Province, and the Yungang Grottoes in Datong, Shanxi Province.

龙门石窟位于河南省洛阳市，开凿于北魏孝文帝年间，直至北宋前后延续四百余年，与甘肃敦煌的莫高窟和山西大同的云冈石窟并称为中国古代佛教石窟艺术的三大宝库。

The Longmen Grottoes is known as a museum of stone carving art. It is not only the artistic expression of Buddhist culture, but also reflects the political, economic and social culture at that time. The Grottoes still contain a large number of historical materials of religion, fine arts, **architecture**②, law, music, dress and personal **adornments**③, and medicine.

龙门石窟堪称石刻艺术博物馆。它不仅是佛教文化的艺术表现，也折射出当时的政治、经济和社会文化。石窟中至今仍然保留着大量宗教、美术、建筑、法律、音乐、服饰和医药等方面的实物史料。

There are 100,000 statues of different sizes in 1,400 caves in the Longmen Grottoes. These works are entirely devoted to Buddhist themes, representing the **pinnacle**① of Chinese Stone Carving Art. Among them, the "Twenty Longmen Products" are the essence of tablet **inscriptions**⑤ of the Northern Dynasties while *The Tablet of Yique Shrine* inscribed by Chu Suiliang is the model of regular **script**⑥ art in the early Tang Dynasty.

龙门石窟的1400个洞穴内有10万座大小不等的雕像。这些作品致力于表现佛教主题,代表了中国石刻艺术的巅峰。其中"龙门二十品"是书法魏碑的精华,褚遂良所书的《伊阙佛龛之碑》则是初唐楷书艺术的典范。

佳句点睛 Punchlines

1. The **excavation**⑦ of the Longmen Grottoes is another large-scale Grotto temple complex dug by the royal family after the Mogao Grottoes in Dunhuang, Gansu Province, and the Yungang Grottoes in Datong, Shanxi Province.

龙门石窟的开凿是继甘肃敦煌的莫高窟和山西大同的云冈石窟之后,由皇室开凿的又一个大型石窟寺群。

2. The Longmen Grottoes began to be built in the **reign**⑧ of Taihe in the Northern Wei Dynasty, and went through the Eastern and Western Wei Dynasties, the Northern Qi Dynasty, the Northern Zhou Dynasty,

the Sui and Tang Dynasties, the Five Dynasties and the Song Dynasty.

龙门石窟从北魏太和年间开始营建,历经东西魏、北齐、北周、隋唐、五代和宋代。

3. In 2000, the Longmen Grottoes was included in *The World Cultural Heritage List* by UNESCO.

2000年,龙门石窟被联合国教科文组织列入《世界文化遗产名录》。

情景对话 Situational Dialogue

A: Have you ever heard of the Longmen Grottoes?

B: Yes, I have. The Longmen Grottoes is located in the south of Luoyang City, Henan Province. It is regarded as the three most famous ones in China, together with the Mogao Grottoes and the Yungang Grottoes.

A: When you stand at the bottom of the grottoes and look up at the giant Buddha above, you would suddenly feel how great human beings are.

B: Yeah, human beings are really amazing.

A: Do you know about Myriad Buddha Cave?

B: Just a little. It completed in 680, is a typical cave of the Tang Dynasty with two rooms in front and back, and a flat-top square. It is a typical building of Tang Dynasty, named after more than 15,000 small

Buddha statues **chiseled**③ on the north and south walls of the cave.

A: Great!

B: We'll visit and tour there sometime.

A: 你听说过龙门石窟吗?

B: 我听说过。龙门石窟坐落于河南省洛阳市南,和云冈石窟、莫高窟一起被誉为中国最著名的三大石窟。

A: 当你站在石窟下面仰望上方的大佛时,就会顿悟人类是多么伟大。

B: 对,人类真是太厉害了。

A: 你知道万佛洞吗?

B: 我知道一点。万佛洞于680年完工,前后两室,有一平顶广场,是典型的唐代建筑。它因洞内南北两壁雕刻的15000多尊小佛像而得名。

A: 太棒了!

B: 咱们有时间一定要去那里参观旅游。

生词注解　Notes

① treasure trove /trəʊv/　*n*. 宝藏;宝库

② architecture /ˈɑːkɪtektʃə(r)/　*n*. 建筑风格;建筑艺术

③ adornment /əˈdɔːnmənt/　*n*. 装饰;装饰品

④ pinnacle /ˈpɪnəkl/　*n*. 高峰;尖峰

风景名胜

⑤ inscription /ɪnˈskrɪpʃn/　*n.* 刻印文字；碑文

⑥ script /skrɪpt/　*n.* 连写体；文字系统

⑦ excavation /ˌekskəˈveɪʃn/　*n.* 挖掘；发掘

⑧ reign /reɪn/　*n.* 君主统治时期；主宰期

⑨ chisel /ˈtʃɪzl/　*vt.* 雕；凿

青城山和都江堰

Mount Qingcheng and Dujiangyan Irrigation[①] System

导入语 Lead-in

青城山是中国道教发源地之一,位于四川省成都平原西北部都江堰渠首工程南侧,因常年青翠、群峰环绕、形状如城而得名,享有"青城天下幽"的盛誉。都江堰是中国著名的古代水利工程,都江堰建成后,成都平原沃野千里,成为"天府之国",如今都江堰已经成为集防洪、灌溉、航运于一体的综合水利工程。青城山都江堰风景名胜是国家5A旅游景区。2000年,青城山与都江堰一起被联合国教科文组织列入《世界文化遗产名录》。

风景名胜

文化剪影　Cultural Outline

Mount Qingcheng, with its back against the snow ridge of the Minshan Mountains, is **verdant**② in all seasons, surrounded by peaks and shaped like a city with winding roads leading to **secluded**③ spots. It is not only one of the birthplaces of Taoism, but also a living "Museum of Taoism". Dujiangyan Irrigation System, located in Guankou Town, Dujiangyan, Chengdu, Sichuan, is known as the "founder of world water **conservancy**④ culture" and a famous tourist attraction in China.

青城山背靠岷山雪岭，四季青翠，群峰环绕，形状如城，曲径通幽，既是道教发祥地之一，也是一座活的"道教博物馆"。都江堰位于四川成都都江堰灌口镇，被誉为"世界水利文化的鼻祖"，是全国著名的旅游胜地。

Dujiangyan Irrigation System headwork is mainly composed of three main projects such as Yuzui, Feishayan and Baopingkou. The three projects cooperate organically, restrict each other, coordinate operations, **divert**⑤ water to irrigate the fields, divide floods and reduce disasters.

都江堰渠首枢纽主要由鱼嘴、飞沙堰、宝瓶口三大主体工程构成，三者有机配合，相互制约，协调运行，引水灌田，分洪减灾。

Built during the Warring States Period, Dujiangyan Irrigation System is not only the world's oldest and only surviving **hydraulic**① engineering, characterized by the absence of dams to channel water, but also a technological milestone in Chinese history, known as "The World's Living Water Conservancy Museum".

都江堰建于战国时期，不仅是全世界迄今为止年代最悠久、唯一留存、以无坝引水为特征的宏大水利工程，也是中国历史上的一个技术里程碑，被誉为"世界活的水利博物馆"。

佳句点睛　Punchlines

1. Pines, cedars, cypresses and various fragrant bushes in the forest form a deep green world on Mount Qingcheng.

森林中的松树、杉树、柏树和各种香灌木丛在青城山上组成了一个深绿色的世界。

2. Dujiangyan Water Conservancy Project is the only existing irrigation project with no dam but can divert water for irrigation **automatically**⑦.

都江堰水利工程是世界上现存的唯一一座无坝引水和自流灌溉的水利工程。

3. The establishment of Dujiangyan is based on the premise of not destroying natural resources and making full use of natural resources.

都江堰的创建是以不破坏自然资源、充分利用自然资源为前

风景名胜

提的。

情景对话 Situational Dialogue

A: Welcome to Chengdu.

B: This is our first meeting. I'm glad to meet you.

A: Is this your first visit to China?

B: Yes, it is.

A: There're many places worth visiting here, such as Mount Qingcheng and Dujiangyan. For tourists, Mount Qingcheng is an ideal summer **resort**®. Pines, cedars, cypresses and various fragrant bushes in the forest form a deep green world on Mount Qingcheng.

B: I've heard that Dujiangyan is an ancient water conservancy project?

A: Yes, it was built by Li Bing and his sons. It has been playing the role of flood control and irrigation for over two thousand years.

B: Really? Then I have to take a good look at this amazing project!

A: I wish you have a good time in here. Welcome to Chengdu again if you have a chance.

B: Surely.

A: 欢迎你来成都。

B: 我们是第一次见面,很高兴认识你。

A: 你是第一次来中国吗?

B: 是的。

A: 我们这里有不少值得一看的地方,比方说青城山和都江堰。对游客来说,青城山是一个理想的避暑胜地。森林中的松树、杉树、柏树和各种香灌木丛组成了一个深绿色的世界。

B: 听说都江堰是一个古代水利工程?

A: 是啊,这是李冰父子修建的,两千多年来一直发挥着防洪灌溉的作用。

B: 是吗? 那我得好好看看这项了不起的工程!

A: 祝你在这里过得愉快。欢迎你今后有机会再来成都。

B: 我一定会的。

生词注解 Notes

① irrigation /ˌɪrɪˈgeɪʃn/ *n.* 灌溉;溉水

② verdant /ˈvɜːdnt/ *adj.* 青翠的;翠绿的

③ secluded /sɪˈkluːdɪd/ *adj.* 僻静的;隐蔽的

④ conservancy /kənˈsɜːvənsɪ/ *n.* 保护;环境保护

⑤ divert /daɪˈvɜːt/ *vt.* 使……改道;转接

⑥ hydraulic /haɪˈdrɒlɪk/ *adj.* 水力的;液压的

⑦ automatically /ˌɔːtəˈmætɪklɪ/ *adv.* 自动地;机械地

⑧ resort /rɪˈzɔːt/ *n.* 度假胜地;常去之地

峨眉山和乐山大佛

Mount Emei and Great Buddha in Leshan

 导入语　Lead-in

峨眉山位于四川省峨眉山市，处在北纬30°附近，一山有四季，是著名的佛教名山和旅游胜地，享有"峨眉天下秀""植物王国""动物乐园""地质博物馆"和"佛国天堂"的盛誉，是一个集佛教文化与自然风光于一体的国家级山岳型风景名胜区。乐山大佛，别名"凌云大佛"，为弥勒佛坐像，是唐代摩崖造像的艺术精品之一。乐山大佛是世界最大的摩崖石刻弥勒坐像，一尊巨型睡佛位于岷江、青衣江、大渡河交汇处，是一道绚丽的自然与人文奇观。1996年，峨眉山与乐山大佛一起被联合国教科文组织列入《世界自然与文化遗产名录》。

文化剪影 Cultural Outline

Mount Emei, which stands on the southwestern edge of the Sichuan Basin, is one of the four famous Buddhist mountains in China, known as the "Buddhist Paradise", whose natural heritage is extremely rich, enjoying the reputation of "plant kingdom" "animal haven" and "geological museum". Great Buddha in Leshan is a giant Maitreya statue carved from a cliff stone, **chiseled**① from the mountain according to the terrain, making it the tallest carved stone Maitreya statue in the world.

峨眉山耸立在四川盆地的西南边缘,是中国四大佛教名山之一,被誉为"佛国天堂",自然遗产异常丰富,享有"植物王国""动物乐园"和"地质博物馆"的盛誉。乐山大佛是一尊摩崖石刻造像巨大的弥勒雕像,依照地形刻山而成,是世界上最高的石刻弥勒菩萨雕像。

Mount Emei is magnificent with deep valleys, waterfalls like jade curtains, **surging**② clouds and **lush**③ trees. There are dozens of Buddhist temples on Mount Emei, as well as many exquisite Buddhist treasures in the temples.

峨眉山雄伟壮观,溪谷幽深,飞瀑玉挂,云海涌动,绿树葱郁,享有"峨眉天下秀"的美称。峨眉山上有佛寺几十处,寺内珍藏有许多精美的佛教瑰宝。

风景名胜

Great Buddha in Leshan was built in 713 and completed in 803, lasting about 90 years. The head of the Great Buddha in Leshan is in line with the mount. He steps on the river with his feet, hands on his knees, with his well-balanced body and solemn look, sitting square by the river. Great Buddha in Leshan Scenic Spot, composed of Great Buddha in Leshan, Mount Lingyun, Mount Wuyou, Reclining Great Buddha and other scenic spots, is a national 5A tourist **attraction**①.

乐山大佛于713年开凿,803年竣工,历时90年左右。乐山大佛头与山齐,脚踩大江,双手抚膝,体态匀称,神情肃穆,临江危坐。乐山大佛与凌云山、乌尤山、巨形卧佛等景点组成的乐山大佛景区是国家5A级旅游景区。

佳句点睛 Punchlines

1. As one of the four famous Buddhist mountains in China, Mount Emei boasts of its magnificence and elegance.
峨眉山壮丽优雅,是中国著名的四大佛教名山之一。

2. Great Buddha in Leshan integrates the charm of the surrounding mountains and rivers into a whole.
乐山大佛集周围的山脉和河流的魅力于一体,浑然天成。

3. Mount Emei is one of the holy places for tourism, **recuperation**⑤ and summer vacation in China.

峨眉山是中国旅游、休养和避暑的胜地之一。

情景对话　Situational Dialogue

A: Do you know about Mount Emei?

B: Yes, I know. I first knew it from television.

A: Mount Emei is one of the four most famous Buddhist mountains in China. The Golden Summit of Mount Emei is an ideal place to view the sunrise, the sea of clouds, Buddha's Glory and **sacred**⑥ lamps.

B: It must be very beautiful.

A: Surely, by the way, have you ever heard of Great Buddha in Leshan?

B: Of course. It's the world's largest stone-carved Buddha.

A: The Buddha faces Mount Emei across the river and at its back is the western slope of Mount Lingyun. A water drainage system reduces **erosion**⑦ by rain and slows **weathering**⑧.

B: I think that's why it has been so well preserved.

A: I learned from the book that a nine-bend plank road was built from the bottom to the top on the right side of the statue, now known as the "nine-bend plank road".

B: So it can be admired up close.

A: 你知道峨眉山吗？

风景名胜

B：是的，知道。我是通过电视知道的。

A：峨眉山是中国最有名的四大佛教名山之一。峨眉山金顶是观日出、望云海、瞧佛光、赏圣灯的理想之地。

B：一定很漂亮。

A：那是当然。顺便问一下，你知道乐山大佛吗？

B：当然，它是世界上最大的石刻佛像。

A：佛像面朝峨眉山，背朝凌云山西坡。排水系统减少了雨水侵蚀，减缓了风化。

B：我想这就是大佛保存如此完好的原因。

A：我从书上了解到，在雕像右边修建了一条从底部到顶部的九弯栈道，现在被称为"九弯栈道"。

B：所以人们能近距离地欣赏大佛。

生词注解　Notes

① chisel /ˈtʃɪzl/　　vt. 凿；雕

② surging /ˈsɜːdʒɪŋ/　adj. 风起云涌的；涌动的

③ lush /lʌʃ/　adj. 苍翠繁茂的；郁郁葱葱的

④ attraction /əˈtrækʃn/　n. 游览胜地；吸引力

⑤ recuperation /rɪˌkuːpəˈreɪʃn/　n. 恢复；复原

⑥ sacred /ˈseɪkrɪd/　adj. 神圣的；庄严的

⑦ erosion /ɪˈrəʊʒn/　n. 侵蚀；腐蚀

⑧ weather /ˈweðə(r)/　vt. 使……风化；使……受风吹雨打

大足石刻

Dazu Rock Carvings

 导入语　Lead-in

大足石刻位于重庆市大足区境内,是唐末宋初宗教摩崖石刻,以佛教题材为主,儒道造像并存,是著名的艺术瑰宝、历史宝库和佛教圣地。大足石刻多层次、多角度,丰富多彩,千姿百态,保存完好,充分代表了9至13世纪世界石窟艺术的最高水准,被誉为"东方艺术明珠"。大足石刻也是世界八大石窟之一,与敦煌莫高窟、云冈石窟、龙门石窟和麦积山石窟齐名。1999年,以宝顶山、北山、南山、石门山和石篆山为代表的大足石刻被联合国教科文组织列入《世界文化遗产名录》。大足石刻是国家5A级旅游景区、全国重点文物保护单位和重庆十大文化符号，2018年荣登中央广播电视总台2018《魅力中国城》文化旅游魅力榜。

文化剪影 Cultural Outline

Dazu Rock Carvings, founded in 650, passed through five dynasties and flourished in the Southern and Northern Song dynasties, covering the **bas-reliefs**[①] on **precipices**[②] of Mount Bei, Mount Baoding, Mount Nan, Mount Shimen and Mount Shizhuan in Dazu County. Well-known for their large scale, exquisite carvings, richness, **diversity**[③] and **intactness**[④], they are the representative of the late grotto art in China.

大足石刻始建于650年，历经五代，盛于两宋，涵盖大足县境内北山、宝顶山、南山、石门山和石篆山的摩崖造像，以规模宏大、雕刻精美、千姿百态和保存完好而著称，是我国晚期石窟艺术的代表。

Dazu Rock Carvings gather the essence of Chinese Buddhism, Taoism, and Confucian statue arts, with **distinctive**[⑤] nationalization and life characteristics, pushing the life of grotto art to an **unprecedented**[⑥] level and becoming a bright pearl in Chinese grotto art.

大足石刻集中国佛教、道教、儒家造像艺术的精华，以鲜明的民族化和生活化特色，把石窟艺术生活化推到了空前的境地，成为中国石窟艺术中一颗璀璨的明珠。

Dazu Stone Carvings have countless **figures**[7] and numerous social life scenes, as well as a large number of written records. They are vivid historical pictures that have made important contributions to the innovation and development of Chinese stone carving art, with **irreplaceable**[8] historical, artistic and scientific values.

大足石刻既有无数人物形象和众多社会生活场面，又有大量文字记载，是一幅生动的历史画卷，对中国石刻艺术的创新与发展作出了重要贡献，具有前代石窟不可替代的历史、艺术和科学价值。

 佳句点睛 Punchlines

1. Dazu Rock Carvings are the best-preserved grottoes in the Chinese Grotto Art Group.

大足石刻是中国石窟艺术群中保存最完好的石窟。

2. Mount Bei Rock Carvings are known as "the exhibition hall of Chinese Guanyin statues" and "a jewel on the crown of Chinese grotto art".

北山石刻被誉为"中国观音造像的陈列馆"和"中国石窟艺术皇冠上的一颗明珠"。

3. In 1999, Dazu Rock Carvings were included in *The World Cultural Heritage List* by UNESCO.

风景名胜

1999年,大足石刻被联合国教科文组织列入《世界文化遗产名录》。

情景对话 Situational Dialogue

A: Do you know about Dazu Rock Carvings?

B: Yes, I do. It's in Chongqing, a beautiful mountain city.

A: You know that. It's amazing.

B: Once I enjoyed a **fantastic**① performance known as Goddess of Mercy with a thousand arms. So amazed I was that I searched online.

A: What did you find?

B: I find that there is the thousand-armed Guanyin on Mount Baoding, which is part of Dazu Rock Carvings.

A: I heard that the social life scenes reflected in the cliff statues of Mount Baoding are **all-inclusive**②, quite like a folk-custom gallery in the Song Dynasty.

B: Maybe we can visit Dazu Rock Carvings next summer vacation.

A: That's a good idea.

A: 你知道大足石刻吗?

B: 我知道,它在美丽的山城重庆。

A: 你居然知道,真是太让人惊讶了。

B: 我曾经看过一场精彩表演,叫千手观音。所以我去网上搜了搜。

A: 那你发现了什么呢?

B: 我发现了宝顶山有千手观音,而宝顶山正是大足石刻的一部分。

A: 我听说宝顶山摩崖造像反映的社会生活情景几乎包罗万象,颇似宋代的一座民间风俗画廊。

B: 我们下个暑假也许可以去那里参观。

A: 好主意。

生词注解　Notes

① bas-relief /ˌbæs rɪˈliːf/　*n.* 浮雕;浅浮雕

② precipice /ˈpresəpɪs/　*n.* 悬崖;绝壁

③ diversity /daɪˈvɜːsəti/　*n.* 多样性;多元化

④ intactness /ɪnˈtæktnəs/　*n.* 未受损伤;完整无缺

⑤ distinctive /dɪˈstɪŋktɪv/　*adj.* 有特色的;与众不同的

⑥ unprecedented /ʌnˈpresɪdentɪd/　*adj.* 史无前例的;空前的

⑦ figure /ˈfɪɡə(r)/　*n.* 重要人物;人影

⑧ irreplaceable /ˌɪrɪˈpleɪsəbl/　*adj.* (因贵重或独特)不能替代的;失掉(或损伤)后无法补偿的

⑨ fantastic /fænˈtæstɪk/　*adj.* 极好的;极出色的

⑩ all-inclusive /ˌɔːl ɪnˈkluːsɪv/　*adj.* 包括一切的;无所不包的

风景名胜

莫高窟

The Mogao Grottoes

导入语 Lead-in

莫高窟,俗称"千佛洞",位于河西走廊西端甘肃省敦煌市,开凿于敦煌城东南鸣沙山东麓的崖壁上,南北全长1680米,有735个洞窟、4.5万平方米壁画和2415尊泥质彩塑,是世界上现存规模最大、历史最久、内容最全、保存最好的佛教和石窟艺术宝库。彩塑是敦煌艺术的主体,彩塑有圆塑、浮塑和影塑等,最高34.5米,最低2厘米,题材丰富,惟妙惟肖,多姿多彩,堪称佛教彩塑博物馆。1961年,莫高窟被国务院列为第一批全国重点文物保护单位之一。1987年,莫高窟被联合国教科文组织列入《世界文化遗产名录》。

文化剪影　Cultural Outline

The Mogao Grottoes, commonly known as the "Thousand-Buddha Caves", are located at the eastern foot of Mount Mingsha, southeast of Dunhuang City, Gansu Province. They were built in the period of the Sixteen Kingdoms, with five rows of caves **distributed**① around. It is the largest and longest preserved Buddhist art treasure house in the world.

莫高窟,俗称"千佛洞",位于甘肃省敦煌市东南鸣沙山东麓,始建于十六国时期,洞窟分布前后左右各五排,是世界上规模最大、保存最久的佛教艺术宝库。

The Mogao Grottoes, located in a **strategic**② point of the Silk Road, is not only a **transit**③ station for trade between the east and the west, but also a **junction**④ of religion, culture and knowledge. It reflects the civilization of the Silk Road and is a huge classical art heritage.

莫高窟地处丝绸之路的一个战略要点,不仅是东西方贸易的中转站,也是宗教、文化和知识的交汇处。它反映了丝绸之路的文明,是一份巨大的古典艺术遗产。

In the Mogao Grottoes of Dunhuang, **frescoes**⑤ are the largest in number and the most **comprehensive**⑥ in content, and they are the only ones in the world. The frescoes of Dunhuang are known as "The Library on the Wall".

敦煌莫高窟的壁画数量庞大，内容丰富，在世界上独一无二。敦煌壁画被称为"墙壁上的图书馆"。

 佳句点睛　Punchlines

1. The Mogao Grottoes in Dunhuang are a shining pearl on the Silk Road.

敦煌莫高窟是丝路之路上的一颗璀璨明珠。

2. The Mogao Grottoes have witnessed the development of ancient Chinese civilization since the Sui, Tang and Song Dynasties.

莫高窟壁画见证了隋、唐、宋以来中国古代文明的发展历程。

 情景对话　Situational Dialogue

A: Do you know Dunhuang?

B: Yes, I do. It's in Gansu Province.

A: Is there anything interesting in Dunhuang?

B: The Mogao Grottoes are the most famous historic interest and scenic beauty.

A: When was it **chiseled**①?

B: The first grotto was chiseled in 366. These grottoes were chiseled over a period of more than one thousand years through ten dynasties.

A: That's really amazing.

B: As you can see, the grottoes are row after row, row above row, forming a five-story massive structure in some places, which are a really wonderful work.

A: It's really **spectacular**®!

B: Yes, I like it so much.

A：你知道敦煌吗？

B：我知道，它在甘肃省。

A：敦煌有什么好玩儿的吗？

B：最有名的名胜古迹是莫高窟。

A：莫高窟是什么时候开凿的？

B：第一个石窟是366年开凿的。这些石窟的开凿历经十个朝代，前后长达一千多年。

A：这真让人惊讶。

B：你们可以看到，成排的石窟层层叠叠，有些竟然达到五层楼高，真是巧夺天工。

A：真是壮观极了！

B：是啊，我太喜欢莫高窟了。

风 景 名 胜

生词注解 Notes

① distribute /dɪˈstrɪbjuːt/ vt. 散布；分配

② strategic /strəˈtiːdʒɪk/ adj. 战略上的；战略的

③ transit /ˈtrænzɪt/ n. 运输；运送

④ junction /ˈdʒʌŋkʃn/ n. 交叉点；接合点

⑤ fresco /ˈfreskəʊ/ n. 壁画；湿壁画

⑥ comprehensive /ˌkɒmprɪˈhensɪv/ adj. 综合的；广泛的

⑦ chisel /ˈtʃɪzl/ vt. 凿；雕

⑧ spectacular /spekˈtækjələ(r)/ adj. 壮观的；引人入胜的

丽江古城

The Old Town of Lijiang

导入语 Lead-in

丽江古城位于云南省丽江市古城区,是纳西族聚居区。自古以来,丽江古城就是远近闻名的集市,它是中国历史文化名城中唯一没有城墙的古城。古城建筑深受纳西族、白族、藏族和汉族建筑艺术的影响,古城内的街道依山傍水修建,以红色角砾岩铺成,有四方街、木府、五凤楼、丽江古城大水车、白沙民居建筑群和束河民居建筑群等景点,具有纳西族的独特风情。丽江古城是中国以整座古城申报世界文化遗产获得成功的古城之一,1997年被联合国教科文组织列入《世界文化遗产名录》。

文化剪影 Cultural Outline

The Old Town of Lijiang is an area **inhabited**① by Naxi people, used to be a trade gathering point on the Ancient Tea-Horse Road, known as the "four best-preserved ancient towns", along with Langzhong in Sichuan, Pingyao in Shanxi and Shexian in Anhui.

丽江古城是纳西族聚居区,曾是茶马古道上的一个贸易集结点,与四川阆中、山西平遥、安徽歙县并称为"保存最完好的四大古城"。

The Old Town of Lijiang is the only Naxi Autonomous Region in China, with a majority of Naxi people. The ancestors of the **ethnic**② minorities in the southwest border built an ancient town without **ramparts**③ on the wonderful land of Lijiang. The simple consciousness of the unity of nature and man and the profound cultural **connotation**④ are integrated into the architecture of the ancient city.

丽江古城里的居民以纳西族同胞为主,是中国唯一的纳西族自治区。西南边陲的少数民族先人在丽江这片奇丽的土地上筑起了一座没有城墙的古城。天人合一的古朴意识和博大精深的文化内涵融入古城的建筑之中。

The Old Town of Lijiang differs from other ancient Chinese cities in terms of architecture, history and the cultural traditions of its native Naxi people. Lijiang is full of beautiful natural scenery. A large number of ethnic minority **compatriots**⑤ provide a variety of rich and colorful culture for visitors to experience. Historically, Lijiang was also known as the "city of love".

丽江古城在建筑、历史及其原住民纳西族的文化传统方面不同于中国其他古城。丽江的美丽自然风光无处不在。众多的少数民族同胞提供了各式各样、丰富多彩的文化供游客体验。历史上,丽江还以"爱之城"而闻名。

佳句点睛 Punchlines

1. The architecture in the Old Town of Lijiang is deeply influenced by the architectural arts of the Xi, Bai, Tibetan and Han people, teeming with a strong flavor of Chinese culture.

丽江古城里的建筑深受西族、白族、藏族和汉族建筑艺术的影响,充满了浓厚的中华文化气息。

2. The unique geographical location, historical background and multiracial inhabitants make Lijiang one of the special old towns.

独特的地理位置、历史背景和多民族的居民构成使丽江成为独具特色的古城之一。

3. The Naxi classical music has always been **hailed**⑥ as the "living **fossil**⑦ of music".

纳西族古典音乐一直被誉为"音乐的活化石"。

风景名胜

情景对话 Situational Dialogue

A: Where did you go last week?

B: I went touring Lijiang, Yunnan.

A: I watched a TV program about the Old Town of Lijiang. It is really an amazing place.

B: Yes. I cannot agree more. The streets in the ancient town of Lijiang are built by the mountain and water, paved with red **breccia**®, which has the unique style of Naxi people.

A: Wow. Is it a mountainous area?

B: Yes. The Old Town of Lijiang is situated on the flatland formed by rivers and surrounded by mountains. It is the only one that combines the architectural styles of north and south in China.

A: Well, I'll be sure to go there and **feast**® my eyes on it when I get the chance.

B: That's it.

A: 上周你去哪里了？

B: 我去云南丽江旅行了。

A: 我之前在电视上看到过有关丽江古城的节目，那里真是美得惊人。

B: 是的，我同意。丽江古城内的街道依山傍水修建，以红色角砾岩铺成，具有纳西族的独特风情。

A: 哇,那地方也是山区吗?

B: 是的。丽江古城坐落在河流冲积平原上,四周环山。丽江古城是中国唯一一座结合了中国南北方建筑风格的古城。

A: 好的,我有机会一定去那里饱饱眼福。

B: 这就对了。

生词注解　Notes

① inhabit /ɪnˈhæbɪt/　*vt.* 栖息;居住于……

② ethnic /ˈeθnɪk/　*adj.* 种族的;人种的

③ rampart /ˈræmpɑːt/　*n.* 土城墙;防御土墙

④ connotation /ˌkɒnəˈteɪʃn/　*n.* 内涵;含蓄

⑤ compatriot /kəmˈpætrɪət/　*n.* 同胞;同国人

⑥ hail /heɪl/　*vt.* 称赞;热烈欢迎

⑦ fossil /ˈfɒsl/　*n.* 化石;顽固不化的人

⑧ breccia /ˈbretʃɪə/　*n.* 角砾岩;角砾石

⑨ feast /fiːst/　*vt.* 尽情欣赏;饱餐

风景名胜

拉萨布达拉宫历史建筑群

The Historic Complex of the Potala Palace in Lhasa

导入语 Lead-in

拉萨布达拉宫历史建筑群位于西藏自治区拉萨市西北的红山上,是一个规模宏大的宫堡式建筑群,包括布达拉宫、大昭寺和罗布林卡。布达拉宫是藏传佛教(格鲁派)的圣地,被称为"世界屋脊的明珠"。拉萨布达拉宫历史建筑群是西藏大型宫堡、园林和寺庙建筑组合的最杰出代表,是藏民族与中国其他各民族以及周边其他文化区域交流与融合的结晶,是雪域高原文化珍品的保存地和著名非物质文化遗产的传承场所。1994年,拉萨布达拉宫被联合国教科文组织列入《世界文化遗产名录》。大昭寺和罗布林卡先后于2000

年和2001年加入布达拉宫世界遗产组合，更名为"拉萨布达拉宫历史建筑群"。

 文化剪影 Cultural Outline

The Potala Palace is regarded as a model of Tibetan **architecture**[①], Jokhang Temple is a typical Tibetan Buddhism temple and Norbulingka is a masterpiece of Tibetan art. The Historic Complex of the Potala Palace in Lhasa is a glorious masterpiece of human imagination and creativity in terms of design, decoration, and harmony with the **environmental**[②] landscape.

布达拉宫被誉为西藏建筑的典范，大昭寺是一座典型的藏传佛教寺院，罗布林卡是西藏艺术的杰作。布达拉宫历史建筑群在设计、装饰，以及与环境景观和谐相融方面都是人类想象力与创造性的辉煌杰作。

"Potala" is a Sanskrit **transliteration**[③], which means "Sacred Land of Buddhism". The Potala Palace is the highest and largest palace-like building complex in the world, known as the "Pearl of the Roof of the World". The palace walls are red-and-white and the palace roofs are magnificent, reflecting the unique characteristics of ancient Tibetan architecture.

"布达拉"是梵语音译，意为"佛教圣地"。布达拉宫是世界上海拔最高、规模最大的宫殿式建筑群，被誉为"世界屋脊的明珠"。宫墙

风景名胜

红白相间,宫顶金碧辉煌,体现了藏族古建筑独有的特色。

The Historic Complex of the Potala Palace in Lhasa is exquisite in architecture, novel and unique in design, rich and **diverse**④ in decoration, and **harmoniously**⑤ integrated with natural beauty. It is not only a symbol of the great creativity of the Tibetan people, but also a unique human cultural heritage on the Snowy **Plateau**⑥.

拉萨布达拉宫历史建筑群的建筑精美绝伦,设计新颖独特,装饰丰富多样,与自然美景和谐统一。它既是西藏人民巨大创造力的象征,也是独一无二的雪域高原上的人类文化遗产。

佳句点睛 Punchlines

1. The Potala Palace is an outstanding representative of Tibetan architecture and the essence of ancient Chinese architecture.

布达拉宫既是藏式建筑的杰出代表,也是中华民族古建筑的精粹。

2. The Potala Palace merges with the mountains, towering and **majestic**⑦.

布达拉宫与山浑然一体,高耸入云,巍峨壮观。

3. The scale and artistic value of the Historic Complex of the Potala Palace represents the highest level of Tibetan architecture.

布达拉宫历史建筑群的规模和艺术价值代表了西藏建筑的最高水平。

 情景对话 Situational Dialogue

A: Have you ever been to the Potala Palace before?

B: No, I haven't. It will be the first time for me to visit it. I've heard it's **spectacular**②.

A: Yes. The stone-and-wood structured Potala Palace consists of the White Palace and the Red Palace. The former comprises halls, temples and courtyards, while the latter includes **stupas**③.

B: I've heard there're eight stupas in the Red Palace, aren't there?

A: Yes. Among these, one is 14.85 meters tall and inlaid with pearls and jades.

B: Really? Then I'll feast my eyes on this sacred place honored as the "Shining Pearl of the Roof of the World" and fully enjoy the extraordinary Tibetan customs.

A: I believe you will surely make this trip worthwhile.

B: Thank you for your blessings.

A: 你以前去过布达拉宫吗?

B: 没有,这是我第一次计划去参观,听说它十分壮观。

A: 是的,石木结构的布达拉宫分为白宫和红宫,白宫由大厅、庙宇和庭院组成,红宫内有佛塔。

风景名胜

B: 我听说红宫内有八座灵塔,是吗?

A: 是的,其中一座灵塔高14.85米,塔内还嵌有珍珠宝石呢。

B: 是吗? 那我得饱饱眼福,看看这个被誉为"世界屋脊的明珠"的圣地,好好领略一下不同凡响的西藏风情。

A: 相信你一定会不虚此行。

B: 谢谢你的吉言。

生词注解 Notes

① architecture /ˈɑːkɪtektʃə(r)/　*n.* 建筑风格;建筑式样

② environmental /ɪnˌvaɪrənˈmentl/　*adj.* 环境的;有关环境的

③ transliteration /ˌtrænzˌlɪtəˈreɪʃn/　*n.* 音译;直译

④ diverse /daɪˈvɜːs/　*adj.* 多种多样的;形形色色的

⑤ harmoniously /hɑːˈməʊniəsli/　*adv.* 和谐地;调和地

⑥ plateau /ˈplætəʊ/　*n.* 高原;(发展、增长后的)稳定期

⑦ majestic /məˈdʒestɪk/　*adj.* 宏伟的;庄严的

⑧ spectacular /spekˈtækjələ(r)/　*adj.* 壮观的;引人入胜的

⑨ stupa /ˈstuːpə/　*n.* 舍利塔;圆顶佛塔

鼓浪屿国际历史社区

Gulangyu International Historical Community

 导入语　Lead-in

　　鼓浪屿,原名"圆沙洲",别名"圆洲仔",南宋时期名为"五龙屿",明朝改称"鼓浪屿",位于福建省九龙江入海口。岛屿西南海滩上有一块礁石在浪潮拍击时音如擂鼓,人们称之为"鼓浪石",鼓浪屿因此得名。鼓浪屿是厦门最大的一个屿,与厦门岛上的厦门大学等隔海相望。鼓浪屿世界文化遗产地范围包括鼓浪屿全岛及其近岸水域,鼓浪屿缓冲区涵盖邻近的大屿和猴屿,并延伸至厦门岛海岸线。在传统聚居地基础上,鼓浪屿逐渐形成了多元文化交融发展的历史国际社区。2017年,鼓浪屿历史国际社区被联合国教科文组织列入《世界遗产名录》,这也是中国第一项海岛世界遗产。

文化剪影　Cultural Outline

Gulangyu Island is a small island with an area of 1.78 square kilometers, located in the southwest of Xiamen City, Fujian Province, enjoying the reputation of "the garden on the sea". The **heritage**① on the island includes 931 historical buildings while the architectural style, natural landscape, historical roads and gardens are **compatible**②.

鼓浪屿位于福建省厦门市西南,是一个只有1.78平方千米的小岛,享有"海上花园"的美誉。岛上遗产包括931座历史建筑,建筑风格、自然景观、历史道路和花园兼容并蓄。

There are multi-national **consulates**③ built on Gulangyu, as well as churches, **mansions**④, foreign banks, schools and so on, known as the "world architecture **expo**⑤".

鼓浪屿上建有多国领事馆,还建有教堂、公馆、洋行和学校等,被称为"万国建筑博览"。

The buildings on Gulangyu Island are compatible with local, Southeast Asian and Western styles, showcasing the blending of ancient ideas and modern life concepts. At the same time, it is also a unique "**pedestrian**⑥ island" in China.

鼓浪屿上的建筑兼容本地、东南亚和西式风格的特点,展现出古代思想与现代生活概念的水乳交融。同时,它还是全国独一无二的"步行岛"。

佳句点睛 Punchlines

1. Gulangyu Island is famous for its natural scenery, cultural **accumulation**⑦ and architecture of all nations.

鼓浪屿因自然风光、文化积淀和万国建筑而闻名。

2. Gulangyu Island is honored as the "cradle of musicians" and the "island of music".

鼓浪屿被誉为"音乐家的摇篮"和"音乐之岛"。

3. Gulangyu Island is a model of multicultural exchange, **collision**⑧ and mutual learning.

鼓浪屿是多元文化交流、碰撞和相互学习的典范。

情景对话 Situational Dialogue

A: We're gonna visit Gulangyu Island, known as the "garden on the sea".

B: The "garden on the sea"! I'm looking forward to going to the dream world.

A: Wow, this shape is like a **tripod**⑨ piano. How pretty!

B: Yes, it's also known as the "island of pianos". Many residents on the island are music fans and play musical instruments such as piano and violin, and many Chinese famous musicians were born here.

A: I want to go to Sunshine Rock. Why was it named Sunshine Rock?

B: Because every morning, the sun rises from here when Xiamen is still in the night, this piece of rock is bathed in the sunshine earliest, so it was named Sunshine Rock. It's the highest peak in that area so we can get a **panoramic**⑩ view of Xiamen.

A: I'll take photos there.

B: OK.

A: 我们要去拜访有"海上花园"之称的鼓浪屿。

B: "海上花园"！我非常期待去那个梦幻世界。

A: 哇,这个岛的形状就像一架三脚架钢琴。太漂亮了！

B: 是的,它有"琴岛"之称,岛上许多居民都喜爱钢琴和小提琴,很多中国著名音乐家都诞生于此。

A: 我想去日光岩,它为什么叫日光岩呢？

B: 因为每天早晨太阳从这里升起,当厦门还是夜晚的时候,这片岩石最早沐浴在阳光下,所以叫日光岩。那里是鼓浪屿最高峰,能将厦门风光尽收眼底。

A: 我一定要在那里留影。

B: 好的。

生词注解 Notes

① heritage /ˈherɪtɪdʒ/ n. 遗产；传统

② compatible /kəmˈpætəbl/ adj. 兼容的；能共处的

③ consulate /ˈkɒnsjələt/ n. 领事；领事馆

④ mansion /ˈmænʃn/ n. 大厦；宅邸

⑤ expo /ˈekspəʊ/ n. 世博会；大型国际博览会

⑥ pedestrian /pəˈdestrɪən/ n. 行人；步行者

⑦ accumulation /əˌkjuːmjəˈleɪʃn/ n. 积聚；累积

⑧ collision /kəˈlɪʒn/ n. 碰撞；冲突

⑨ tripod /ˈtraɪpɒd/ n. 三脚架；三脚桌

⑩ panoramic /ˌpænəˈræmɪk/ adj. 全景的；远景的

澳门历史城区

The Historic Center of Macao

导入语 Lead in

澳门历史城区以澳门旧城为中心,贯通相邻的广场和街道,包括妈阁庙前地、亚婆井前地、岗顶前地、议事亭前地、大堂前地等二十多处历史建筑。历史城区的范围东起东望洋山,西至新马路靠内港码头,南起妈阁山,北至白鸽巢公园。澳门历史城区是中国境内现存最古老、规模最大、保存最完整、最集中的中西特色建筑共存的历史城区,是四百多年来中西文化交流、多元共存的结晶。2005年,澳门历史城区被联合国教科文组织列入《世界文化遗产名录》。

文化剪影 Cultural Outline

The Historic Center of Macao, located in Macao Special Administrative Region, China, is comprised of twenty-two buildings on the Macao Peninsula and eight **adjacent**① front grounds. It is the oldest, most intact and concentrated building complex coesisting with the Eastern and Western styles in China.

澳门历史城区位于中国澳门特别行政区,由二十二处位于澳门半岛的建筑物和相邻的八块前地组成,是中国境内现存最古老,保存最完整、最集中的东西方风格共存的建筑群。

As the first **territory**② set up by a European country in Eastern Asia, it is an important witness to the spread of Western religious culture in China and the Far East. The Historic Center of Macao has witnessed a history of more than 400 year's multicultural of coexistence and mutual exchange of culture between China and the West.

作为欧洲国家在东亚建立的第一个领地,澳门历史城区是西方宗教文化在中国和远东地区传播历史的重要见证,见证了澳门四百多年来中西方文化多元共存的历史。

The Historic Center of Macao is the oldest **extant**③ Western architectural heritage in China and a comprehensive embodiment of Eastern and Western architectural art. The historic buildings in Macao also carry the characteristics of Eastern and Western cultures reflecting the **integration**④ of Eastern and Western cultures.

澳门历史城区是中国现存最古老的西式建筑遗产,是东西方建筑艺术的综合体现。澳门的历史建筑同时承载了东西方文化的特点,反映了东西方文化的相互交融。

佳句点睛 Punchlines

1. The Ruins of St. Paul is one of the landmark buildings in Macao, and also one of the "eight sights of Macao".

大三巴牌坊是澳门的标志性建筑物,同时也是"澳门八景"。

2. Macao's "historical city proper" is a unique treasure, which is one of the representative **evidences**⑤ of the integration of Chinese and Western cultures in China.

澳门的"历史城区"是独一无二的瑰宝,是中西文化在我国相互融汇的代表性印证之一。

3. Macao is located in the convenient location of land and sea **transportation**⑥, where Chinese and Western cultures blend and **radiate**⑦ outward.

澳门处于海陆交通的便利位置,中西方文化在这里交融后向外辐射。

情景对话 Situational Dialogue

A: Do you know why we call it Macao? It has nothing to do with its **Mandarin** and Cantonese pronunciation.

B: Actually, the English name comes from the local belief in Mazu. It is a misunderstanding.

A: Can you tell me more about it?

B: Yes, I can. In 1553, the place where the Portuguese landed was near the Mazu Temple, which in Macao was called "Mage Temple". The Portuguese asked the local people, "What's the name of this place?" The local people thought that they asked about the name of that area, so they answered, "Mage." Thus Macao became a Macau by mistake.

A: Oh, I see. Do you have any Macao attractions to recommend?

B: Lou Kau Mansions, which is the home of **prominent** Macau merchant Lou Kau in the early twentieth century. It is the architectural style of a typical Chinese-style mansion in the gentle and delicate period of the late Qing Dynasty.

A: Okay, I'll visit it.

B: I hope you'll have a pleasant trip to Macao.

A: 你知道为什么澳门叫"Macao"吗？这与它的普通话发音和粤语发音都没有关系。

B: 这个英文名源于当地信奉的妈祖。其实是一个误会。

A: 可以说详细一点吗?

B: 好的,1553年葡萄牙人登陆的地方在妈祖庙附近,而澳门的妈祖庙叫"妈阁庙",葡萄牙人问当地人"这里叫什么",当地人以为他们问那片区域叫什么,便回答"妈阁",于是澳门就这么阴差阳错地变成"Macao"了。

A: 噢,我知道了,你有什么推荐的澳门景点吗?

B: 卢家大屋是澳门二十世纪初商人卢九的住宅,具有晚清时期典型的柔和雅致的中式大宅的建筑风格。

A: 好的,我会去那里的。

B: 希望你的澳门之行愉快。

生词注解 Notes

① adjacent /əˈdʒeɪsnt/ *adj.* 相邻的;邻近的

② territory /ˈterətri/ *n.* 领土;版图

③ extant /ekˈstænt/ *adj.* 尚存的;现存的

④ integration /ˌɪntɪˈɡreɪʃn/ *n.* 融合;一体化

⑤ evidence /ˈevɪdəns/ *n.* 证据;证明

⑥ transportation /ˌtrænspɔːˈteɪʃn/ *n.* 运输系统;运输工具

⑦ radiate /ˈreɪdieɪt/ *vi.* 辐射;流露

⑧ Mandarin /ˈmændərɪn/ *n.* 普通话

⑨ prominent /ˈprɒmɪnənt/ *adj.* 显著的;卓越的